THE

Boston Merchants

AND THE

Non-Importation
Movement

Charles McLean Andrews

THE

Boston Merchants

AND THE

Non-Importation

Movement

RUSSELL & RUSSELL

New York

FIRST PUBLISHED IN THE TRANSACTIONS OF
THE COLONIAL SOCIETY OF MASSACHUSETTS, VOLUME XIX, 1916-1917
NOW FOR THE FIRST TIME ISSUED AS A SEPARATE VOLUME
IN 1968 BY RUSSELL & RUSSELL
A DIVISION OF ATHENEUM HOUSE, INC.
BY ARRANGEMENT WITH THE ESTATE OF CHARLES MC LEAN ANDREWS
AND THE COLONIAL SOCIETY OF MASSACHUSETTS
L. C. CATALOG CARD NO. : 67-18290
PRINTED IN THE UNITED STATES OF AMERICA

THE

Boston Merchants

AND THE

Non-Importation
Movement

I

The mercantile activities of such prominent colonial towns as
Boston, Newport, New York, and Philadelphia are factors to be
reckoned with in colonial history, for the mercantile houses and or-
ganizations were the American agencies concerned with the promotion of trade and commerce, and the trading interests of British
merchants had a decided influence upon the governmental policies
of the day and often directed the actions of council and parliament.
Trade, in itself considered, may be deemed a sordid human activity,
lacking the glamor of war and diplomacy, a selfish pursuit, drab and
unadorned, but it is one of the highly developed organic functions
of the social system, representative of a more advanced stage of
social evolution than is agriculture, and in its operations offering
many explanations of historical events, the causes of which have
frequently been sought elsewhere. The doctrines and enterprises
of the merchants of the eighteenth century, both in England and
America, are conspicuous to a noteworthy degree, and often play a
leading part in determining our external relations, but they do not

become historically visible until the period immediately preceding the Revolution, when they take on great political importance. They are apt to be passed over, however, with only a brief mention in our histories. Sons of Liberty and Committees of Correspondence find ample recognition, but where will one discover any attempt to glorify the origins of our Chambers of Commerce? Yet the latter deserve as careful a study as do the former, for many of them arose out of an organized effort to meet the difficulties which we were called upon to face in our controversy with the mother country.

Boston from early times was the home of merchants, who as business men, adventurous spirits, and writers on trade became prominent in colonial history. Zachariah Gillam and his son Benjamin, John Nelson, Samuel Waldo, Charles Lidgett, Thomas Banister, Joshua Gee, Andrew Belcher, Sr., Charles Apthorp, and others were leaders in activities that carried them beyond the confines of the colony into the larger commercial world. But there is no special reason to think that during this early period they and their fellow merchants acted together in any organized fashion for the protection or promotion of trade. Protests there were and community of action in regard to custom-house affairs, and it is possible that even before 1751 they had begun to meet in a more or less regular way for the advancement of their common interests, but of continued and concerted coöperation there is no sign.

About 1750, however, in the days when Sir Harry Frankland was collector of the port on the British establishment, friction arose owing to the latter's fondness for seizing ships concerned in illegal trade, and we find a petition signed by fifty-three of the merchants of Boston, protesting against a proposed appointment to the court of vice-admiralty. The period was one of concern to the traders, some of whom had suffered from royal impressments and all had been outvoted in town meetings, where, as Shirley claimed, it was irksome for them to attend, and they had fallen into the convenient habit of petition in matters which directly concerned their interests. It was at this time that they began to gather in the front room toward the Long Wharf of the British Coffee House, the tavern kept by Cordis and Mrs. Cordis [1] on the north side of King Street, to

---

[1] Cord Cordis married (for his second wife) Hannah Jones (widow of Elnathan Jones), October 2, 1740; and died at Concord, aged 63, July 29, 1772. His

consider questions of trade. How often these meetings were held we cannot say. Probably then, as later, this Merchants' Club met frequently, informally, and without call, the members dropping in when they liked, and varying in number from half a dozen to twenty-five or thirty according to the weather, other engagements, and the exigencies of trading conditions. No records were kept and no references are to be found to the meetings.[1]

But in 1763, the need of more definite organization was felt. The end of the long war had come, peace had been anticipated for many months, the terms of the settlement had been in a measure already made known, and fears had been aroused of a renewal of the Molasses Act, which was due to expire the next year. Consequently on April 14, 1763, the members of the Club came together and resolved to organize themselves into a Society.[2] They appointed a committee to draw up "some general rules and orders for their government" and a few days later this committee reported the following articles:

That the Company form themselves into a Society, by the name of The Society for encouraging Trade and Commerce within the Province of Massachusetts Bay

That this Society shall consist of Merchants and others concerned in Commerce and of any other Persons of Ability and Knowledge in Trade who may be desirous to encourage the same,

That there shall be a General Meeting of the Society sometime in the month of April or May annually, to consider the state of Trade and

---

widow died in London in 1779. (Boston Record Commissioners' Reports, xxviii. 214; Wyman, Genealogies and Estate of Charlestown, i. 240; Boston News Letter, August 6, 1772.)

[1] It is more than likely that the Club was behind the movement of 1761 to oppose the writs of assistance and to break down the whole vice-admiralty system in Boston. Two of its members, Harrison Gray, treasurer of the province, and John Erving, one of the council, were plaintiffs in suits before the common law courts against vice-admiralty officials, which were designed, as Governor Bernard said, "to destroy the court of admiralty and with it the custom house which cannot subsist without it." (Colonial Office, 5:891, Ll 67, 68; Beer, British Colonial Policy, 1754–1765, pp. 119–123.)

[2] In the original document the year is not given, and there is no mention of the founding of the Society in contemporary newspapers or diaries, but as John Hammock, Jr., one of the signers, died January 7, 1764 (Boston Gazette, January 16, 1764), and John Simpson, another of the signers, died June 30, 1764, while on his way from Fayal to Philadelphia (ibid. July 30, 1764), the year must be 1763. Furthermore the object of the Society was to prevent the renewal of the Molasses Act, and we have records of its activity in December, 1763.

to determine upon any matters relative thereto that shall be laid before them, and that the particular Day of such meeting shall be appointed by the Standing Committee for the time being,

That at the General Meeting a Chairman shall be chosen by written vote (the greatest number of Votes to determine the choice) whose Business shall be to moderate at the meeting and put the questions, to be determined by vote. At such meeting a clerk also shall be chosen to minute down the Proceedings and record the votes of the Society.

That business may be carried on with greater decency and order, any Member who may have anything to propose, shall address himself to the Chairman and care shall be taken to avoid, as much as possible, all Party disputes and every thing that may tend in any measure to dissolve the Union of the Society, or to interrupt the good harmony which ought to subsist among the members of it.

That at the General Meeting annually, there shall be a Standing Committee chosen, consisting of [fifteen [1]] of whom [9 [1]] shall be a quorum. The Members of which Committee shall be chosen singly by written vote, the majority of voters to determine the choice.

That the Committee shall meet together Monthly (or oftener, if they see cause) to consult upon the affairs of Trade, to take notice of anything which may be judged prejudicial to it, and to receive any Proposals that may be made for its advantage; and shall make Report of the same to the General Meeting, to be acted upon there as shall be judged proper.

That the Standing Committee (if they think there is sufficient reason therefor) may occasionally call a General Meeting of the Society at which Meeting the Business shall be regulated and carried on, in the same manner as at the stated annual meetings.

That upon Request in writing subscribed by Twenty or more of the members (without assigning any special reason) the Committee shall call a General Meeting.

That the Committee, either in the Public News Papers or some other way, as they shall judge most proper, shall cause notice to be given of the Time and Place of the General Meetings two days at least before the Same.

That any Persons of other Towns in the Province who are friends to Trade and desirous to advance the interest thereof, and who may be in Town [2] at any Time when the Standing Committee meets, may be invited to be present with them.

---

[1] In another hand.

[2] Crossed out in the original.

4

~~That if any of the Standing Committee should become a Member or Members of the General Court, he or they shall thenceforth cease to be of the Committee.~~[1]

That at every General Meeting each member present shall before he departs leave with the Clerk [a pistareen [2]] or whatever the Company shall deem sufficient in order to defray the Expences of the Meeting: and the Clerk shall account with the Society for what he receives.

That the Tavern Expences of Committees shall be born by themselves, but all other charges which may be incur'd for the Service of the Society, shall be defreyed by the whole [an account of which shall be laid before the Society at their annual meeting [2]].

That every person who shall subscribe his name to the foregoing articles shall be deemed a member of the Society.[3]

These articles are signed by one hundred and forty-six merchants, a number of whom must have been members of the Merchants' Club for many years, while others were doubtless sons of those who in 1750 had signed the petition to the Treasury. Two at least were from distant towns, one from Nantucket and one from Falmouth (Portland). In the years that followed, many others joined the Society, while some of those whose names are recorded doubtless fell away in the strenuous days of the non-importation controversy.

Thus the organization of the merchants took on three forms. First, the Club, an informal body, which had been in existence since 1751, meeting regularly at the British Coffee House, the Bunch of Grapes, or less frequently at the [Admiral] Vernon's Head,[4] and there indulging in much talk and considerable liquor, wine and punch, for which each person paid his own charge,[5] and there too having debates and controversies over trade, sometimes acrimonious.[6] The members dropped in as they pleased, always in the evening, and there were rarely present less than five, or more than twelve. There

---

[1] Crossed out in the original, with a marginal note "not passed."

[2] In another hand.

[3] Massachusetts Historical Society, O2517, a collection of papers originating with the Society for the Promotion of Trade and Commerce and gathered by Edward Payne, secretary of its Standing Committee.

[4] Drake, Old Boston Taverns, pp. 33–38, 38–39, 55, and Appendix.

[5] Rowe, Diary, March 25, 1767.

[6] William Molineux was one of the chief offenders: see Rowe, February 11, 1768, and Drake, pp. 41–43, for a Molineux-Otis anecdote. Molineux was known and disliked as an agitator.

5

was no formal procedure or taking of minutes, though sometimes an understanding was reached to request the Committee to meet and consider some important business. Among those recorded as attending most frequently, during the period from 1764 to 1770, are Joshua Winslow, Harrison Gray, Thomas Gray, John Boylston, Nicholas Boylston, Edward Payne, Captain Davis, John Erving, Jr., William Molineux, Melatiah Bourne, Samuel Hughes, Thomas Brattle, James Otis, James Perkins, Isaac Smith, Jeremiah Gridley, Ezekiel Goldthwait, James Warden, and Benjamin Hallowell. Some of those attending stayed only an hour, while others remained for the greater part of the evening. Secondly, the Standing Committee of fifteen members, of whom nine constituted a quorum, which met at one of the taverns, monthly or oftener, if necessary, considered the general conditions of trade and prepared business for the larger body. The hour was usually, but not always, in the morning. John Rowe was the first chairman and Joshua Winslow his successor, and Edward Payne was secretary. The membership included Thomas Cushing, John Hancock, Thomas Gray, John Erving, Jr., William Phillips, Deacon John Barrett, and others whose names have not been preserved. At these meetings states of the trade were drawn up, grievances presented, and remedies contrived, and decisions were reached to call a general meeting at a certain time and date. No minutes were kept, as far as the evidence goes to show, but the secretary took down the main conclusions, making rough drafts which he afterwards copied out in fair hand. The members of the Committee, as of the Club, bore their own tavern expenses, but charges arising from business undertaken in the interest of the Society as a whole were met from the common purse.[1] Thirdly, the General Meeting, or as it was also called, the Whole Body, the Body, or the Trade, which met annually under the rules, probably in May,[2] and had a

---

[1] Thomas Gray and Edward Payne had been instructed to draft a state of the trade in 1763, and to make every effort possible to prevent a renewal of the Molasses Act. In doing so, they incurred considerable expense, for which under the rules of the Society they should have been reimbursed. That this was not done appears from their statement to the Committee in January, 1766, that even "if the Society that remains should pay them half a dollar each for the purpose aforesaid there would even then be a deficit" (Massachusetts Historical Society, O2517).

[2] Boston Evening Post, May 14, 1764: "The annual meeting of the Society

dinner; but in the years from 1766 to 1771 it met much more frequently, though we cannot always tell whether a meeting was composed of the members of the Society, the subscribers to the agreements, or the merchants and traders at large, that is, the merchants and traders and others concerned in trade, as the phrase went. That the Society suffered diminution of numbers after the Stamp Act controversy is evident, but how far this affected its procedure and activities is not clear. For a subscribers' meeting, notices were sent out on little printed slips, varying in size at different times, evidently according to the printer's convenience, signed by the chairman of the Committee and addressed to the subscriber.[1] For an open meeting, the call was sometimes published in the newspapers and sometimes announced on printed slips without signature or address. As far as recorded the numbers present at these meetings varied greatly. From thirty to one hundred were present at the subscribers' meetings, and we are told that as many as a thousand attended an open meeting at Faneuil Hall. At the meetings special committees were appointed [2] and resolutions adopted. John Rowe, from whose diary [3] we obtain considerable information about these various meetings, was a zealous attendant until the excesses of the non-importation party, in 1769 and 1770, dampened his enthusiasm and curtailed his attendance, and for a time he ceased to go altogether. On the occasion of an important meeting, April 25, 1770, he had gone fishing.

The society thus organized for the promoting of trade and commerce was the first board of trade for the city of Boston, and was the forerunner of the Chamber of Commerce founded in 1785. Its

---

for encouraging Trade and Commerce will be held this evening at the British Coffee House. The members are desired to give their attendance."

[1] Massachusetts Historical Society, Broadsides.

[2] Such as that of March 1, 1768, to correspond with merchants in other trading towns and provinces and consisting of John Hancock, John Rowe, Edward Payne, William Phillips, Thomas Boylston, Arnold Welles, Melatiah Bourne, Henderson Inches, and John Erving, Jr. A committee was also appointed to prepare a list of those articles which it might be thought necessary to import, and there were doubtless many others.

[3] This diary was first published, with some omissions, in 2 Proceedings Massachusetts Historical Society, x. 60–108; later in a separate volume (called Letters and Diary) edited by Mrs. Cunningham, in more complete form. I have been carefully over the original manuscript and obtained therefrom much additional information regarding the meetings and those who were present at them.

origin was probably due to the reports, sent to the colony by the agent, Jasper Mauduit, of new proposals regarding trade under consideration in England, and probably also to warnings given to the merchants in Boston by their correspondents in England, who were always prompt to discover whatever was mooted in Board of Trade, Privy Council, or parliament likely to affect the American trade. Charles Townshend was appointed first lord of trade on February 23, 1763, but it is unlikely that letters announcing his policy could have been received in Boston before April 14 and so have influenced the founding of the Society on that date. As the immediate purpose of the Society was to prevent the renewal of the Molasses Act, its first task was to draft a "State of the Trade," in which the burdens of that act, as far as they concerned New England, should be adequately presented. The business was placed in the hands of Thomas Gray and Edward Payne, as a sub-committee of the Standing Committee, who entered into correspondence with the merchants of Marblehead, Salem, and Plymouth, requesting them to furnish information about the fishery and to send committees to consult with the sub-committee in Boston.[1] In consequence of the information thus received, the Society in December, 1763, drew up a memorial, containing a statement of reasons, and presented it to the General Court. Marblehead, Salem, and Plymouth each did the same.[2] The General Court referred the four memorials to a

[1] The New York merchants were equally active at this time. In February, 1764, they assembled in the Long Room of Burn's tavern, which as a merchants' meeting place corresponded to the British Coffee House in Boston, and appointed a committee to prepare a memorial to the assembly of the province, representing the decline of trade and the distresses of the merchants and traders of the city. This committee, which may be the same as that noted below, p. 174 note 2, wrote to Philadelphia advising the merchants there of their intention of "heartily joining the eastern governments in soliciting a discontinuance of the most unjust of all laws, the Sugar Act," and of requesting the assembly to instruct the agent in England "to go hand in hand with the other governments." Apparently the merchants of Rhode Island did the same, for the assembly there in February, 1764, ordered a memorial regarding the duties on sugar, molasses, etc., "to be sent to Mr. Agent Sherwood" (Boston Gazette, February 13, 1764; Boston Evening Post, March 26, 1764). It would be interesting to know more about this early instance of coöperation among the merchants. I owe these references to Miss Viola F. Barnes, who made the search for me.

[2] Massachusetts Historical Society, O2517, no. 17. Memorial of Merchants and Traders of Boston, "That a certain Act of Parliament in the sixth year of his late Majesty's reign, generally known by the name of the Sugar Act [Mo-

committee of both houses, with instructions to prepare a letter to Mauduit, which was done. On February 10th, the merchants forwarded their statement, with a letter, to the regular agent, William Bollan, and at the same time transmitted copies to all the neighboring colonies and placed two hundred and fifty in the hands of the merchants of London for distribution. Bollan received the letter on April 10th, five days after the Sugar Act became a law. The "State of the Trade" he never received at all, so that the first effort of the Society to meet the new British policy ended in failure.[1]

---

lasses Act], being near Expiring, they have the greatest reason to expect that the W. Indian planters will use their utmost endeavours to procure the renewal of it" (Massachusetts Archives, Court Records, xxv. 100. Memorial of Merchants and Traders of Plymouth, xxv. 100; of Marblehead, xxv. 109; of Salem, xxv. 114). Unfortunately the General Court proceedings, from December 21, 1763, to January 24, 1764, with all supplemental papers, were burnt in the fire which destroyed Harvard Hall on the night of January 24, 1764, where the assembly was sitting on account of the epidemic of small-pox in Boston. These letters and memorials were among the papers lost. But the committee was instructed to recover what it could, to prepare a letter to Mauduit during the recess of the assembly, and to place it in the hands of the Secretary for despatch (xxv. 143, 152–153, 194).

[1] The text of the "State" probably contained the following sections:

One principal branch of the trade of this province is the fishing carried on to the Banks; in this branch there is upwards of 300 vessels employed, besides a great number of small boats in the Bay, and in the Mackrel Fishing about 90, the Fish these vessels cure, with the pickled Fish and Liver Oyl amounts to upwards of £160,000 stg. per annum; — about ⅔ of this Bank Fish turns out merchantable and is sent to Spain, Portugal, and Italy, the net proceeds of which with the freight is remitted to Great Britain; the other ⅓ being such as is oversalted, sunburnt, and broken, and thereby rendered unfit for any market in Europe is sent to the Islands in the West Indies, first to the English Islands, which cant consume more than ⅓, the remaining ⅔ is sent to the French foreign islands, in return for which we receive Molasses and a small proportion of ordinary sugars. This valuable branch of trade and nursery of seamen almost if not wholly depends on our trade to the foreign islands in the West Indies (as we cannot cure fish for the European market separate from the other sort sent to the West Indies) and as we have no other Market for what is made by the Bankers, it will be lost if not sent to the foreign islands in the West Indies and this loss must infallibly destroy the whole bank fishing.

Another considerable branch of our trade is lumber of all kinds which is sent to the West Indies, also provisions, horses, onions, and many other articles suitable for the West Indies, in which trade there is upwards of 300 vessels employed in this province. Most of these vessels call first at the English islands (who

II

From 1764 to 1768, except for a brief period following the date for the enforcement of the Stamp Act, the members of the Merchants' Society devoted themselves very largely to the one great task of convincing the authorities in England that the new acts of revenue and trade were not only a burden to the colonies but a menace to Great Britain herself. They endeavored to show, in all sincerity, that the acts of 1764, 1765, and 1766 were certain to obstruct trade and in the end to ruin it, and that whatever threatened the prosperity of America threatened that of Great Britain also, affecting the well-being of the British merchant and the revenue accruing to the British Exchequer.

They began by saying that the colonies were able to pay for British manufactures in only three ways: either by what they produced

---

consume but a small proportion of what we export). When they are supplied, the remainder is carried to the foreign islands.

Some oak timber and staves are sent to Ireland, some to Madeira and the Western Islands to purchase wines, and some few cargoes are sent to Spain, Portugal, and England, but none to any foreign port to the N° of Cape Finisterre; as the first cost of these cargoes of lumber is very small, the whole profits are no more than a freight for the vessel, but this freight is a great encouragement to ship-building, a very considerable branch of trade in this province, where there has been upwards of —— built in a year, before the late embarrassments were laid on our trade since wch this number has been reduced ⅓.

Some of these ships with fish, oyl, potash and naval stores are sent direct to Europe, but chiefly to the West Indies with lumber, fish, and other articles of our produce, the proceeds of which with the freight to England, together with the vessel, are remitted to Great Britain to pay for the goods we receive from thence, and by having timber plenty and building so many vessels we become carriers for all other parts of America besides the trade to the West Indies. Many of our ships go to Virginia, N° and S° Carolina, where they carry large quantities of rum and other northern produce to purchase rice, tobacco, and naval stores, and take in freight for Great Britain where the Proceeds of the whole and indeed of all our trade centers (Massachusetts Historical Society, O2517).

I have not had access to a copy of the "State" of 1763, if such exists. Probably that sent to the General Assembly was lost in the fire. The figures given above correspond to those furnished by Marblehead and Salem, and the statement above, though containing a reference to the Sugar Act of 1764, and so actually written after that date, is likely to be nothing more than the earlier one adapted to a new need. Many such "States" were drafted between 1763 and 1769 and the same wording appears throughout. New "States" are simply old "States" added to. A copy of the "State" has recently been found: see pp. 379–390, below.

10

among themselves, by what they caught out of the sea, or by the money or commodities obtained in "a circuity of commerce abroad," and they argued that whatever diminished this purchasing power, by lessening the trade of the colonies or otherwise, was bound to be prejudicial to Great Britain.[1] This lessening of the trade was seen in the restrictions imposed on the export of foreign sugar (from the foreign West India islands) and on the liberty to export, after being warehoused in a colonial port, directly to a foreign market, such as Holland, Hamburg, or Petersburg. Were such restrictions removed, they said, it would encourage colonial trade in foreign sugars, which might in time become considerable and increase the remittances to Great Britain, "whereas under the present regulations none will ever be brought here [Boston] in order to be reported to a foreign market in Europe." They objected to the restraints placed upon the molasses trade, which "is a great spring to every branch of business among us, such as the fishing, the lumber trade, and shipbuilding, because molasses is distilled into rum, as well as our trade to Africa."[2] They likewise objected to the restraints placed upon

---

[1] In studying the grievances of the New England merchants we must remember that New England had four particular forms of economic activity — agriculture, fishing, commerce, and manufactures, in the last three of which she was the rival of Great Britain. The southern colonies and the West Indies had neither manufactures, commerce, nor fisheries. See American Husbandry, i. 434–435, ii. 236–245.

James Bowdoin wrote to Alexander Mackay, November 29, 1770: "What is remitted to England is by a circuitous trade, and principally from Spain & Portugal, all which added to the numerous articles of their own and foreign produce sent by them to Britain is scarcely sufficient to pay for what they import from thence. Whatever, therefore, is taken from them as revenue not only so far prevents the paying the debt due to Britain, but operates to the discouragement and lessening of their general trade, upon which their ability to pay that debt and continue that importation depends" (6 Massachusetts Historical Collections, ix. 242).

Franklin wrote to Peter Collinson, April 30, 1764: "We are in your hands as Clay in the Hands of the Potter and so in more particulars than is generally considered, for as the Potter cannot waste or spoil his Clay without injuring himself so I think there is scarce anything you can do that may be hurtful to us, but what will be as much or more so to you. Does anybody see that if you confine us in America to your own Sugar Islands for that commodity, it must raise the price of it in England. Just so much as the price advances, so much is every Englishman tax'd to the West Indies" (British Museum, Add. MSS. 37021, f. 21).

[2] William Barrell proposed to ship sugar from St. Croix to Boston, consigned to his brother Joseph Barrell. The latter warned him that the duties must be

the export of foreign logwood, which was obtained "by small cargoes of provisions produced among us, together with some British manufactures, which has employed many vessels, but now being obliged to carry it first to England, it will incur heavy expences by reason of its bulk, and so there will be an end to this business." They asked for direct importation of oranges, lemons, and all kinds of fruit, as also oil consumed in the fisheries, partly to save the great expense, port charges, and delay involved in stopping at an English port, and partly to avoid the danger to perishable articles of a long voyage. The expense, they said, exceeded the amount of the duty, and delays destroyed a commodity which had "become almost a necessity for the health and comfort of the inhabitants of North America." They hoped that parliament would permit the direct importation of the wines of Spain and Portugal also, because the supply of wine from Madeira and the Azores had become insufficient and the price very high, and they could always send their pipe-staves in exchange. They asked to be relieved of the prohibition to send flaxseed,[1] lumber, and potash to Ireland.

Above all, the merchants objected to the multiplicity of bonds required by these acts, in addition to those required by the acts of 1660 and 1672, particularly the bond that lumber should not be landed in any part of Europe north of Cape Finisterre, except Great Britain, and that which prevented rum from being taken to the Isle of Man.[2]

paid ("if you ship anything it must undoubtedly pay the duty"), and said that he would have to get the permission of the governor of the Danish island "which he had never refused to give" (April 12, 1709, Barrell Papers, Library of Congress).

In a letter written to Jasper Mauduit, Nov. 24, 1764, and later sent to Richard Jackson, an unknown correspondent (the Society?) emphasizes the fact that the duties levied by the act of 1764 were a heavy drain on the colony, particularly in the matter of molasses, because the French would suffer none to trade without permits and these permits were very costly; the business had to be transacted by such a person as they appointed, "who was allowed ten per cent for doing it, and he charged the molasses as he pleased and no questions must be asked" (Massachusetts Historical Society, Massachusetts Papers, no. 1: not in the printed collection). Barrell had great trouble with the Danish governor and finally failed to get permission. The Society laid a great deal of stress on these points in its statements. Compare my Anglo-French Commercial Rivalry (American Historical Review, July, 1915, xx. 763 note 6).

[1] The sending of flaxseed to Ireland was a very important aspect of New York and New England commerce at this time. The merchants said that the trade was worth £40,000 a year. See Commerce of Rhode Island, i. passim.

[2] The object of this bond was to prevent smuggling. Until 1765, the Isle of

They quoted instances of coasters giving upwards of twenty bonds in a year, all or most of which were in force at the same time; and they believed that parliament could hardly have foreseen the effect of the acts upon the coasting trade of the colonies, or it would have realized that the cost of the bonds and of the certificates needed to cancel them would amount to more than the first cost of all the lumber sent to Europe. They objected strongly to the unlimited powers given to officers of the customs by the act of 1764, wherein the defendant who lost the suit was entitled to no costs whatever, and to only two pence damages in case he won a suit against an officer for wrongful seizure, whereas if the officer won he recovered triple costs. They objected to the extension of the powers of the vice-admiralty courts, which were —

Empowered to seize any or all the ships or goods of the American merchant at their leisure, and though they act ever so arbitrarily or unjustly the merchant has no remedy, the officer not being subject to any damage or even costs of suit; while the claimer, if he should be non suited or discontinue his action must pay treble costs, if the judge of the vice-admiralty-court shall say there was a probable cause of seizure, which no doubt will always be the case, as not only the officers of the customs but likewise the governor of the province, being interested in those seizures, will always encourage and promote the same, and many instances may be produced where both vessel and goods have been condemned as forfeited only for a mistake or neglect of the master when the revenue has not been affected or any fraud intended, which severities are not imposed on our Fellow subjects in Great Britain, where the Commissioners of the Customs settle all such mistakes where no fraud was designed.

For this reason, the merchants declared, the whole trade of America lay at the mercy of the officers of the customs and the judge of the admiralty court.

Man had been controlled by private lords and in consequence smuggling had gone on to such an extent as to call for governmental interference. The custom-house books of western Scottish ports, notably those of Ayr, show the extent of this clandestine running of rum to Great Britain. In 1765 parliament bought out the governmental rights of the proprietaries, the Duke of Atholl and others, for £70,000, and immediately passed acts regulating the trade of the island. Under these acts the colonists were forbidden to carry rum to the Isle of Man and were required to give a bond not to do so. (5 George III, cc. 26, 39 sections 5, 6, c. 43.)

Besides the bonds, said the merchants, every master of a vessel, even coasters, had to take out a sufferance and a cocquet for every article he took on board, and in case he took any goods for which bond was required he had to have a certificate from the collector of his having given bond, and in case he neglected to take out such certificate, not only the goods but even the vessel and the rest of the cargo were forfeited. Before a cocquet could be taken out for any goods (even of British manufacture), an oath must be taken by whom and in what vessel the article intended to be exported was imported, a thing often impossible. They protested against the "great expence and needless trouble accruing to the Trade by means of a naval officer," who had been appointed originally "for the inspection of trade and the prevention of irregularities and abuses therein," when there were no officers of custom in America, and they begged that this official be dispensed with.[1]

These were the essential features of the grievances of the merchants, which as we can well believe were debated nightly in the rooms at Mrs. Cordis's or Colonel Joseph Ingersoll's or Mr. Thomas Hubbard's, and given more orderly form at the meetings of the Standing Committee. They constituted the chief objections thus far agreed upon for inclusion in the "Proposals to the Parliament for the Regulation of the American Trade," which Thomas Cushing told Dennys De Berdt, the special agent for Massachusetts appointed in 1765, were being prepared by a committee of Boston merchants.[2] But, as it happened, the proposals were not sent in that year. Two new subjects for consideration came up that constituted serious grievances in the eyes of the merchants of New England. In the act of 1766, the duty on molasses was reduced to a penny a gallon, but even this reduction was not satisfactory, as the merchants wished the duty removed entirely, and there can be no doubt that the concessions in

[1] It is difficult to disentangle and classify these various drafts framed by the Standing Committee. No. 26 seems to be of date 1764, with additions of 1767; no. 27 must be of date later than 1766; no. 54 is the first draft of no. 39, which was probably that sent to De Berdt; while nos. 52, 53, 58–60, 65–67, 74, were probably notes used in making up no. 39, the last part of which is contained in nos. 55 and 56. No. 31 is apparently the latest of all, and was completed toward the end of the year 1768, as it embodies all the claims made since 1763. Nos. 68–70 may be the original draft of no. 31.

[2] Thomas Cushing to Dennys De Berdt, June 28, 1766 (Massachusetts Papers, Seventy-Six Society Publications, no. 3, p. 15).

this act and in that of 1765, upon which their friends and correspondents in England sent them congratulations, were in their eyes
largely discounted by the many restrictions which embarrassed the
trade and caused great disappointment.[1]

The second grievance of the year 1766 concerned the cod and whale
fishery, a capital article and of conspicuous national importance,
though deemed by many in England an "improper employment for
colonies and detrimental to the interests of the mother country."[2]
For years the New England fishermen had been charged with breaking the act to encourage the trade to Newfoundland,[3] with debauching
the British sailors with rum, rinding the standing timber of Newfoundland, running an illicit trade with the French there, carrying
off British seamen by offers of higher wages, and generally abusing
the freedom of the fishery, until it could be said that there was "not
one old England ship [in the Labrador fishery] or seaman employed
therein nor a seaman raised thereby for the service of the fleet."[4]
With the appointment of Palliser as commodore-governor in 1764, the
Commissioners of Customs recommended an addition to his instructions calling for an enforcement of the law. Consequently Palliser
in 1765 began his attempt to check the activities of the New England fishermen. For two years [5] these attempts continued until the
merchants could say that —

By the cruisers under this gentleman's command some of the New
England vessels] have been plundered of what fish they had caught,
others have had their best hands pressed, the loss of whom was the occasion of and ended in the entire loss of their vessels; on some they
have inflicted corporal punishment, but all that were in their way were

---

[1] Massachusetts Papers, Seventy-Six Society Publications, no. 3, p. 29.

[2] American Husbandry, ii. 245.

[3] 11 William III, c. 25.

[4] Acts of the Privy Council, Colonial, vi. § 704. Cf. Calendar of State Papers,
Colonial, 1704–1705, § 116; representation of the Board of Trade, April 29, 1765,
Colonial Office, 195: 9, pp. 397–424; and the additional instructions to Palliser
of May 6, 1765, ibid. pp. 434–436. Some of these orders are in the Book of Orders
and Proclamations by Governors of Newfoundland, Public Record Office, Admiralty, Greenwich Hospital, Miscellanea, Various, 121.

[5] Palliser arrived, for the second time, on April 3, 1766, and began to issue rules,
orders, and regulations to be observed on the coast of Labrador. Under these
rules no New Englander was to take cod in the straits of Belle Isle or off the coast
of Labrador.

drove off, by means of which their voyages were broken up and every one was threatened with confiscation of vessel and effects, if they presumed to fish there another year.[1]

When De Berdt wrote to Cushing in September, 1766, he said that he had heard nothing from the merchants, so it is probable that no letters passed between them until January, 1767. Then the committee wrote, forwarding the petition that had been in preparation for several years. They characterized this petition as a "representation of the difficulties which Trade still labors under by means of some late Acts of Parliament." De Berdt had already received a statement of grievances from the General Court of Massachusetts and had laid them before Secretary Halifax, some time in the early summer of 1765, but as Halifax was dismissed in July, he repeated them in a larger memorandum and sent them to Lord Dartmouth, who was appointed first lord of trade in the same month. But it was not until January 17, 1767, that the Society sent over its first petition. To this act it had been prompted by a letter from a committee of the merchants of New York, dated November 24, 1766, saying that "the universal and concurrent opinions of the principal merchants through the Continent, all uniting in material points, must carry conviction," and that they hoped the Boston merchants would not be "behindhand with [them] in their common cause, but like Brethren and fellow-citizens [would] join with [them] in promoting it, uninfluenced by sinister views or private interest." [2]

---

[1] Massachusetts Historical Society, O2517, nos. 55, 56. See also Massachusetts Papers, p. 40, where additional grievances regarding the fishery may be found. In Massachusetts Historical Society, O2517, no. 65, is the following: "Mr. Palliser posted an order in the Town House and sent for the masters of all the vessels belonging to the plantations, forbidding [them] to tarry at St. John's or any of the other harbours after the last day of October [1766], and if any presum'd to tarry after that time they were to have their rudders taken off and their sails carried into the Fort, and likewise sail masters to give bonds with sureties not to bring away any passengers. By which we are entirely excluded from the Cod fishery." Cf. no. 74.

[2] The letter was addressed to James Otis, Benjamin Faneuil, Henry Lloyd, John Rowe, Samuel Hughes, and Stephen Greenleaf, and was signed by John Cruger, John Alsop, James Jauncy, Walter Franklin, Henry White, Richard Yates, Isaac Sears, Robert Murray, Gerard Beekman, David Van Horne, and Elias Desbrosses (Massachusetts Historical Society, O2517, no. 30). For the general situation in New York and for comments on the petition, see Becker, History of Political Parties in the Province of New York, 1760–1776, pp. 28–39.

Actuated by a desire to coöperate and feeling perhaps the need of stating some of their particular grievances, for the New Yorkers said nothing about the fishery, the Society sent its own petition to De Berdt, signed by sixty names, headed by that of Joshua Winslow, and embracing all the points that we have touched upon up to this time. De Berdt, having remarked in his letter of March 9th that "the New York petition had some warm expressions which gave offence to the House," [1] and was ordered to lie on the table, could say in that of March 14th that the Society's grievances were very well stated and decently expressed.[2] Some results were obtained, the restrictions upon the Irish trade had already been removed, and promises were given by Secretary Shelburne and by Commodore Palliser, about to start on his summer cruise to Newfoundland, to look into the grievances regarding the fishery.

But the subjects for debate at the Merchants' Club were not yet complete. In June, 1767, parliament passed three acts, commonly known as the Townshend Acts: one creating an American board of Customs Commissioners, with its seat in Boston, which was to exercise in America the powers formerly possessed by the Commissioners of Customs in England; a second, designated in this paper the Townshend Act, imposing duties on glass, lead, painters' colors, tea, and paper; and a third making certain concessions to the East India Company, which controlled the tea trade. The board, provided for in the first act, was commissioned September 8, 1767, its members reached Boston on November 5th, and held their first session on the 18th, and it was not long before the merchants were ready with a crop of new grievances. They complained of the great increase of restrictions and embarrassments due to the frequent attendance demanded at the collector's office, and the inevitable delays that accompanied it. They objected strongly to the requirement imposed by the board that each shipper make out an exact report of his cargo, without the privilege of post-entries from day to day, as was allowed in Great Britain, and they protested vehemently against the fees, particularly from coasters, due to their being obliged to clear in the same manner as vessels bound on foreign voyages, and to give bond for

---

[1] Massachusetts Historical Society, O2517, no. 74.

[2] Ibid. nos. 34, 35. Printed in Letters of Dennys De Berdt, 1757–1770 (Publications of this Society, xiii. 451–452).

every trifling article they carried for private families, such as a few pounds of tea or sugar or a few gallons of rum or molasses purchased of retailers. Formerly, they said, coasters had not been required to take out cocquets for such articles, and the fees which used to be but a shilling for entering or clearing, were now ten shillings or a guinea, which was "more ready money than they sometimes received for their whole freight." [1]

They complained further of the great number of tide-waiters and inferior officials that were appointed, and of the requirement that masters admit and lodge them under deck, without any authority to do so. Some of these men, they said, were not trustworthy, and the masters and merchants did not think their interests safe under their care. These officers took upon themselves the liberty of searching vessels before they were discharged, and sometimes before the masters had reported at the custom house, an insolent action which was illegal and contrary to the practice in Great Britain. They construed as an "intolerable grievance" the appointment of officers of customs on board the men of war, cutters, and other armed vessels, and the "arbitrary and unlawful manner" in which they exercised this authority in the province, which they deemed "unprecedented in any other part of the British dominion." Some of the officers, by force of arms, had entered vessels on the high seas and in the harbors, demanding of the masters their papers, breaking open the hatches and searching the holds with lighted candles. Even ships from London, with hemp and powder on board, were not exempt, and the lives and properties of the king's subjects had been greatly endangered. Some vessels, they said, coming into the harbor, even before the master could reach the custom house to

---

[1] The fees exacted at the custom houses everywhere at this period were a distinct grievance to the merchants. There were two forms of protest, one against excessive fees, and the other against fees that were illegal or were not authorized at all. On July 31, 1769, fifty-one of the leading merchants of Newport entered into an agreement not to pay higher custom-house fees than the law allowed and to guard strangers against the exactions of the custom-house officials (New Hampshire Gazette, October 13, 1769). The same question came up in Connecticut, when in October, 1769, memorials were presented to the assembly, which disclose the antagonism existing between the merchants and the customs officials (Connecticut Archives, Maritime and Trading Affairs, ii. nos. 90, 91). The protest had been made in the colonies as early as 1764 and was continued till 1770. It was emphatic in Philadelphia and Charles Town.

make report, had been boarded by armed boats from the Romney, and one vessel from the West Indies had had her hatches opened and twenty hogsheads of molasses hoisted upon deck, that the hold might be searched. Another vessel with lumber was carried alongside the Romney, had her hatches opened, and the boards taken on board the king's ship, before the master was permitted to go to the custom house to report. Several other vessels had been seized in the bay, at the Vineyard, and other ports, where they had been obliged by contrary winds to make a harbor, and sent into ports they were not bound for and there detained at great expense on pretence that some trifling articles, belonging to the mariners, and not specified in the cocquet, were to be found on board.

They further complained that upwards of twenty sail of men of war, cutters, and other armed vessels, purchased by the Board of Customs Commissioners, had been employed "to cruize on the Trade of this province," without discovering one vessel engaged in smuggling, "though their expectations were so raised in hopes of plunder that some of the commanders of the king's ships purchas'd small vessels on their own acc't, sent them into the little harbors and coves where the men of war could not cruize," disguising some of them as coasters and employing every device possible to detect illicit and contraband trade. One master —

of a little cutter purchased a fishing boat on his own acc't for the same purpose, but being disappointed of the advantages they expected to reap from the condemnation of the prizes or illicit traders, they have been induced to take advantage of the mistakes and omissions of the masters of coasting vessels, several of whom have been seized by those *guarda costas* and two actually condemned for some trifle found on board without being claimed. Since the arrival of the Commissioners between 20 and 30 vessels have been seized and several masters fined £100 stg. for landing some goods before they had reported at the custom house, four of these were seized by the officers of custom in port and condemned for landing a few casks of wine and molasses more than they had reported; the others seized by the cruisers were dismissed after waiting some time at a great expense, except two coasters, which were condemned for having some trifles on board for which they could produce no cocquet and one open lighter for a small cask of brandy and three boxes of lemons found on board.

Referring to the preambles of the acts, which state that the design was to raise a revenue, the merchants called attention to the fact that even if the amounts expected should be raised, they would not compensate "for the Damages that will arise to the Trade, Navigation, and Fishery of the Colonies and the Manufactures of Great Britain." They continued:

Furthermore to collect this revenue the government has been at a great expence, equal, at least, if not superior to all the revenue that could have been collected had the trade been as extensive as it was before these acts were made, which is not the case now nor never will be while these acts are in force. Besides the vast charge for troops, men of war, and cutters stationed here to prevent any clandestine trade and to support any officers of the customs in putting these acts (which have regularly been submitted to) in execution. Then courts of vice-admiralty are constituted, with a salary of £600 a year to each of the judges, a board of commissioners with a salary of £2500 per annum, also an additional number of Custom House officers appointed by that board, amounting in the whole to near 200, some of whom have salaries from £30 to £50 per annum.[1]

In conclusion, the merchants said in recapitulating their grievances, —

These indulgencies would have a happy tendency to unite Great Britain and her colonies on a lasting foundation; all clandestine trade would then cease, the great expence of men of war, cutters, and custom house officers to secure this revenue be saved; trade, navigation and

---

[1] The colonial grievances against the courts of vice-admiralty at this period reached their climax in the case of Henry Laurens in Charles Town, who had three vessels seized and condemned. Laurens's comments on this event can be found in his pamphlets, for the titles of which see Wallace, Life of Laurens. Some of his views, as given in his Letter Books, are even more expressive. He speaks of "the tyranny of custom house officers . . . the losses from their unjust exactions and from the rigorous, artful, and illegal decisions in the American courts of vice-admiralty . . . the vast extent of jurisdiction and powers given to a single man who may be a fool or a knave or both . . . those rapacious, haughty, insolent and overbearing men, such as our collector was during his short six months residence here, are great troublers of quiet minds . . . such men are the greatest enemies to Britain of any men in America and as one vile priest does more injury to the cause of religion than two rakes, so does one such officer or man in power more prejudice to the interest of Britain in America than twenty mouthing Liberty Boys" (Laurens, Letter Book, iv. 31, 168, 192, 329, 353, 355, 370, 374, South Carolina Historical Society).

fishery would greatly revive, and the demand for British manufactures be very much increased.

There is nothing to show that the merchants sent over a second petition or brought the later grievances to the attention of parliament. By 1768, the movement had begun to take on a new form, a change due largely to the Townshend Act, which as the Boston merchants said in enumerating their grievances did not "affect the Trade in the same manner as the other duties and restrictions." But it did affect the people at large, and for this reason. The revenue and trade acts of 1764, 1765, and 1766, though couched in more elaborate form and laying greater emphasis on the revenue features, were in large part expressive of the old right of parliament to regulate the trade and commerce of the colonies, a right first exercised in the navigation acts of 1660, 1663, 1672, and 1696, and thus were nothing more than extensions of British policy as it had existed for a century. It was natural that these acts should have been objects of resentment to the merchants of Boston, for they were expressly designed to bring within bounds the somewhat untamed trade of the northern colonies. To prevent the passage of these acts was the main purpose for which the Society had been founded. Had the colonists found no other causes for complaint than the grievances which we have presented, then the Revolution would not have occurred, for it is practically certain that on this point a compromise would have been reached that would have satisfied both sides to the controversy. In the year 1767, there was a widespread desire in America for a reconciliation with England and a hope that reconciliation would come.[1] At the same time the

---

[1] Adams, Cushing, Otis, and Gray wrote to Dennys De Berdt, December 20, 1765: "We find that attempts have been made to raise a jealousy in the nation that the colonists are struggling for independence, than which nothing can be more injurious. It is neither their interest, nor have they ever shown the least disposition to be independent of Great Britain. They have always prided themselves on being British subjects" (Adams, Writings, i. 70–71).

Laurens wrote in 1767: "As to our European-American affairs I am under no dread about them, there may possibly be some disagreeable work, but even such work must be soon at an end and produce an establishment of union to endure for ages. There are mistaken men on both sides, the eyes of the nation will be opened and men on either part who do not want wisdom and who can see the compatibility of freedom and subordination will arise with healing under their wings and

statesmen in England were anxious to end the dispute and the British merchants, with but few exceptions, were working in behalf of peace. The latter knew that the trade restrictions were injuring American and Briton alike and felt sure that when once this fact was driven home to the official mind, such modifications would be effected as to calm colonial fears and restore harmony and peace. The Boston merchants themselves said that all they wanted was to return to the situation as it had been before 1764, and had this been all that the controversy involved colonial wishes might have been met.

III

The Sugar Act of 1764 was, as is well known, something more than an act regulating trade and commerce; it was designed also to raise a revenue in America to meet the cost of colonial expansion. This part of the act was due not to the demands of the commercial policy, that is, mercantilism, but to the demands of the new imperialism. Great Britain had emerged from the Seven Years' War an empire, with new territory and with new obligations, and the disposition of this territory and the fulfilment of these obligations became the paramount issues. How to raise a revenue in America was an important though subordinate part of the imperial policy, and was the object in part of the Sugar Act and entirely of the Stamp Act and the Townshend Act. The duties imposed by the first and last of these acts were customs duties, levied on imports from the foreign West Indies in the case of the Sugar Act and from England in the case of the Townshend Act. The taxes imposed by the Stamp Act were of the nature of internal revenue taxes to be paid by every individual who engaged in certain legal transactions or certain forms of business or who bought a newspaper, a pair of dice, or a pack of cards. That the stamp tax promised to be exceedingly onerous, we have ample evidence to show.[1] Had it been enforced it would have

---

build an everlasting bridge from Britain to British America. God grant it may be so" (Letter Book, iv. 52).

[1] William Allason wrote to his brother, September 6, 1765: "We may expect a good collection next spring unless the Stamp Duty should have the same bad consequences that is generally apprehended from it. By all accounts it will drain the country in a few years of all the money in circulation and entirely put it out of the power of people in trade to recover their small debts by the charge of the sheriffs that will be necessary in the prosecution of a suit for a trifling sum, of

affected in one way or another nearly every individual in the colonies, except slaves, indented servants, and children under age. Such a tax was burdensome in itself, quite apart from the constitutional question involved, but it was made far more burdensome to the colonists by the requirement that it be paid in the sterling money of England. This meant not in kind, as was the four and a half per cent of Barbadoes and the Leeward Islands, nor in paper currency, as might be the local colony rates, but in hard money, gold or silver or copper. Now payments in hard money had always been a colonial difficulty, especially in small amounts, because of the scarcity of small coins, and many suggestions had been made in the preceding three quarters of a century looking to the increase of such coins, copper and silver, for colonial use. As early as 1715, Attorney General Northey had expressed the opinion that the plantation duty should be paid in silver,[1] and many efforts had been made to have the quitrents paid in like manner, but without any great success. In all these cases the amounts were trifling as compared with the sum, that would have to be paid under the regulations of the Stamp Act and the Townshend Act.

The years from 1761 to 1769 were a time of severe financial depression in the colonies, trade was dull, money scarce, credit poor, and debt the common burden of farmers, country storekeepers, merchants in the cities, and people generally. There was hardly a

---

which most of our debts consist." He further adds that in case of a suit "the plaintiff cannot recover the Stamp Duty as he can the other costs, since it is not so provided by Parliament" (Allason Papers, Virginia State Library).

[1] Calendar of Treasury Papers, 1714–1719, p. 157. In 1765 Van Cortlandt wrote, "I would order tobacco could part of the duty be saved, but a penny sterlᵍ Duty will not answer" (Letter Book, New York Public Library). It was reported from Charles Town in 1770 that the "Kings duties" were paid in silver, and this term probably included the plantation duty (South Carolina Gazette, May 31, 1770). For the quitrents, see Bond, The Quit Rent System in the American Colonies (American Historical Review, April, 1912, xvii. 508–510). There was probably no hard money to speak of in the interior towns of any of the colonies, certainly not in New England, where scarcity in the cities, due to trade and the fisheries, would involve the country districts, which were entirely dependent on the mercantile centres for cash. For example, Enfield even at this period was making all authorized grants for schools, ministers, and town expenses "to be paid in the produce of the earth" (Allen, History of Enfield, i. 432–443, and passim). A similar condition prevailed in all the agricultural communities of New England.

section of the country from Portsmouth to the tide-water regions of Virginia and North Carolina that did not feel the pinch of this money stringency and where the complaint of bad times was not heard.[1] Prices were low, debts very hard to collect, bonds given had to be sued for in county courts, many persons were sold up by the sheriff and others thrown into jail. We read of men locking themselves in their houses to escape arrest [2] and making the best terms they could with their creditors. Though business had always been done on a credit basis, in a country where money was "hard to come at," as the phrase went, there had never been a time when indebtedness among all classes of the population had run so long or reached such high figures. The country storekeepers, unable to collect from the farmers, could not pay the city merchant who furnished them sugar

[1] "Distress and poverty stalks among us equal to anything among our neighbours" (Letter from New Bern, N. C., June 10, 1768, New Hampshire Gazette, July 22, 1768). The Boston Gazette of November 2, 1767, speaks of "the present alarming scarcity of money and consequent stagnation of trade, and the almost universally increasing complaints of debt and poverty." A Providence town meeting, after listening to the report of its committee on December 4, 1767, stated as a reason for its vote that the colony was heavily in debt, its inhabitants subject to burdensome taxation, trade, which for some years had been on the decline, was suffering under great embarrassments, medium very scarce, and the balance of trade very unfavorable (Providence Gazette, December 12, 1767). Newport made the same statement, December 4 (Boston Gazette, December 14). In 1764, times in New Jersey and Pennsylvania were considered bad by all writers, and failures were not uncommon. On April 5, 1769, Washington wrote to George Mason, "That many families [in Virginia] are reduced almost, if not quite, to penury and want by the low ebb of their fortunes, and that estates are daily selling for the discharge of debts, the public papers furnish too many melancholy proofs" (Life and Correspondence of George Mason, i. 140); and in October, 1769, an address was sent to Gov. Franklin of New Jersey on the "Deplorable State of the Province, arising partly from the excessive scarcity of money and decay of trade, but chiefly from the multiplicity of lawsuits, mostly for debt" (New Jersey Archives, xxvi. 529). This petition led to the passage of the New Jersey Act "For the Relief of Insolvent Debtors." John Watts of New York wrote to Gov. Monckton in 1765, "The illboding aspect of things, cramping of trade, suppression of paper money, duties, courts of admiralty, appeals, internal taxes, etc., have rendered people so poor, cross, and desperate that they don't seem to care who are their masters or indeed for any master" (4 Massachusetts Historical Collections, x. 587, December 30, 1765). See also a letter from J. W. Watts to the same, February 4, 1769, on the situation (Chalmers Papers, iii., New York Public Library).

[2] William Dunterfield of Imlay's Town, Pa., did this in 1767, and Nathaniel Barrell, whose financial troubles split the Sandemanian Church in New Hampshire, locked himself in his house for six weeks in 1766.

24

and rum from the West Indies and manufactured goods from England, while he in turn could not meet the current accounts rendered yearly by the British merchant, and had to shorten his orders or suffer the chagrin of having them refused, because the commission merchants or manufacturers in London, Liverpool, Bristol, or Hull were unwilling to extend further credit.[1]

---

[1] As the point here made is an important one, I should like to substantiate it by quoting a part of the evidence upon which it is based, drawn not from the newspapers but from the merchants' letter-books of the period.

Thomas Browning of Georgetown, Maryland, wrote to Stephen Collins in 1762: "Collections in the Cuntry is I can say with truth the worst I ever knew them (March 15)." "The Farmers are not making more than half crops of wheat and not more in proportion of Indian corn. I can only say that two thirds of our farmers when I call on them for their account say that if we pay you off our children must suffer for bread" (June 15: Collins Papers).

The Allason letters of 1763 are full of references to suits to recover money from debtors in Annapolis, Philadelphia, North Carolina, and the up country. "I believe there never were so many suits depending in this country [Virginia] as there is at this time. Scarcely a prison is allowed to stand [empty] in some counties" (W. Allason to his brother, June 24, 1764, Allason Papers).

John Schaw, writing to Allason on February 9, 1763, said: "I have left above £1500 debts behind me [in Annapolis] and I shall go over about the last of March to make a collection," with the result that "I made a very unsuccessful journey of it myself, I mean in collecting my debts, which gives me great uneasiness. The people there had nothing in short to pay me" (Letter of April 1, 1763). His journey included the Eastern Shore also.

Ezra Collins to Stephen Collins, March, 1763: "Thy old friends Dan¹ King, W. Vane, Jⁿᵒ Nutting of Salem failed thousands worse than nothing."

Scott & Gill wrote to Collins from Boston, April 18, 1763: "There is scarce any other money than gold passing here and a rare thing to see a dollar."

Collins threatened one Thomas Barber of Piles Grove, New Jersey, with an execution until he paid or gave security, and couched his letter "in an angry style." Barber replied that going to prison would not pay the debt.

John Kirkpatrick wrote from Alexandria, November 26, 1764: "I have been abroad these three weeks in quest of money but never met so great disappointment in collection. I had a great dependence on Col. Philip Lee, but in vain. There is £28 due from Col. Wᵐ Fitzhugh in Stafford which I sued for." Parrish wrote from Accomac in 1764: "Times is hard and money hard to collect, at least I find it so" (May 29, 1764), and he calls 1765 "that fatal year," not because of the Stamp Act but because of his business troubles.

The letters from Joseph Barrell to his brother William emphasize constantly his difficulties in raising money, April 15, June 15, 1763. That of April 22 mentions the matter three times.

On May 4, 1765, Peter Schmuck of Hardwick, New Jersey, wrote Collins: "I received thy letter yesterday by which I understand thy uneasiness which I am sorry for and should have come to Town before now if I could got my money in which I have been trying ever since Last Fall but all in vain and now I began to

The current of indebtedness was always toward Great Britain. The farmers were in debt to the country merchants and local store-

sue and it seems to be all one. Of twenty fife person which I suit at one time I got my money only of four and the rest I must get it by execution, which it seems to go very hard. For such times never was known among people for there is never a week but there are some vendues of the sheriffs and constables." In 1767 Collins sold up Schmuck, who wrote him a scornful letter, September 23. Collins in commenting on the situation said, May 21, 1768: "Sheriff, coroner, and I think Schmuck are all dependent on each others Lenity, either having executions against each other or debts due."

Jacob Isaac to Collins: "I am schmd to come without the money becust it has been so long standen" (February 23, 1766). John Milhause to Collins, April 26, 1766, says much the same, and later, November 18, adds that he has enough owing him to pay many bonds but that it is impossible to get it quickly by suing, as the law allows three months in small debts and three courts in large ones. John Sheppard to Collins, June 19, 1765: "I have as much more money owing to me as I owe, but I cannot command it at this time by Rason of the great Scarcity of money." Michael Hessler appealed to him in two letters from "Reading Gaol," August 25, September 2, 1765. Jonathan Bowen of Cohansey, September 5: "I am getting in the money for you as fast as possible." John Long to Collins, Burlington, New Jersey, November 25, 1766: "I rec^d your letter leding me no the Scarcity of money and indeed I put no Dout in it for I can get none at all."

In 1767, William Barrell of Portsmouth was down to bed-rock in the matter of cash. "I havent 5 dollars in the world," he wrote, April 15, 1767.

John Rodermel to Collins, "Richmont townsib, Barks County," Pa., May 2, 1768: "I bake of you dow dwade me six monds lonker Deng will bay you ac whidoud fale den id unbasble for me to bay id sowner. Den I hobe you vont but me in ane chust [jail] dou it is ware hards time to gad money."

In February, 1769, William Allason had twenty-six cases in Fredericksburg County court against Shenandoah debtors, among whom were Daniel Morgan, the Ashbys, and others. His suits, 1762–1764, against persons owing him either on bond or on account numbered 126, as follows: Frederick county 38, Stafford 30, Fauquier 24, Culpeper 16, etc. In 1768–1770, the total number was 94, covering fourteen counties and the general court. Allason kept a list of his lawyers (Allason Day Book and Suit Book).

The financial difficulties do not appear to have been as serious in New York as in Pennsylvania, though Philip Van Cortlandt said in 1764 that trade was "almost intirely stopt by the severity of the customs officers and men of war," and his letter-books show that he had considerable sums owing him in Virginia, which he could not get except at serious loss. "I could wish the gentlemen of Virginia had been as punctual in payments as I have been in answering their requests," he writes, and his correspondence is as spicy as is that of Collins. He had to go to law in some cases and to threaten to do so in others. As to his own business, he says, "I do but little more than pay the expence of my works at present," and in December, 1765, speaks of "these dull times, the distressed situation, little business done, no law in force, a terable time." "Most of the sugar houses are stopt since last Fall," he writes in March, 1765, a situation due of course to the Sugar Act, the scarcity of raw sugar, and the watchfulness of the custom keepers, the latter to the city merchants and wholesale importers, and they in their turn to the commission merchants and manufacturers in England. While it is true that a great deal of business was by barter and exchanges in kind, yet book balances had to be settled in money, either paper or cash in America and cash or bills of exchange in England, that is, in sterling. Book debts [1] were not available as assets and notes as a rule were not accepted. In the colonies credit ran generally from four to six months, while between England and the colonies the period was from nine to twelve months, after which interest was charged. In making payment in England, coin — generally dollars, sometimes gold—was shipped in bulk, or bills of exchange were sent, and these had to be bought with cash, for unless a merchant had a balance of his own in England he had to purchase a bill of other merchants who acted as brokers, and such bills were always difficult to obtain in small amounts and sometimes could not be obtained at all or only at high rates of exchange.

The period we are considering furnishes ample evidence of the difficulties which the merchants in America had to meet their debts in England. One concrete illustration, in no way exceptional or peculiar, is of more value, however, than many generalizations. I take the following quotations from the Collins Papers, to which reference has already been made.

---

house officers and men of war. In 1768, he reported sugar again as low and other sugar houses as "stopt in the city." From John Van Cortlandt's ledgers may be obtained figures regarding the suits against Roscoe Sweny and Col. Tucker of Virginia, and Abraham Maers of North Carolina, as well as ample additional evidence of debts due all the way from New Haven to Hampton, Virginia.

[1] Book debts play a very important part in colonial business and were the subject of legislation in a majority of the colonies. They occupy much space in ledgers after 1758, but comparative estimates are difficult to reach, on account of the scarcity of evidence. John Glassford, a well-known Scottish merchant, with a string of stores along the Potomac and near-by waters, enters in one of his ledgers a list of 250 customers with debit and credit items (October 1, 1760). The customers owed him £125 stg, 1613 lbs tobacco, and £975 Virginia currency; he owed them £15 stg, 3426 lbs tobacco, and £54 Virginia currency (Firm Accounts, Maryland and Virginia, v. Library of Congress). The entering of debts in a merchant's ledger is no sign of specially bad times, but the following in ledgers of the period under consideration may be noted: "Debts deemed Desperate," "Insolvent Debts," "Dead and no Effects," "Denies the Debt," "Sued," "Run to Virginia" (many), "Lunatick and no Effects," "No such man can be found," "Lost by Judgment." It should be noticed that "Desperate Debts" was the customary term for bad debts (Mair, Bookkeeping Modernized, p. 516).

On July 13, 1762, Neate and Pigon wrote: "We have lately been so extremely badly remitted from Phil[a] that it puts it out of our power to give such extensive credits. . . . It greatly hurts us not to be paid in time . . . consider what must become of us to be detained out of One hundred thousand pounds perhaps for many months after the Invoice is due. Our Capital is not large enough and indeed times have been so bad that no fortune in England can support such credits."

On February 13, 1763, they complained of "the backwardness of our friends in your city in their payment," and on February 18, 1765, pointed out that Collins owed them £1024, "now all considerably overdue" (March 14, 1765), some of it of three years' and some of it of two years' standing. "It is an unreasonable credit and such which requires the Bank of England to support," and on January 1, 1766, they wrote for £699, "being in much distress for money." Mildred and Roberts, to whom Collins owed £3037, wrote, a few months later, "Though the money may be safe in thy Hands, yet it will not pay our debts here and Interest is no Equivalent to the Disappointment in our Trade." [1]

Collins was a conscientious man of business and as early as 1763 reduced his orders, hoping to strike a balance.[2] He was "fearful of not being able to remit in due time," though he was encouraged to think that trade would "a little revive." But he was disappointed. In 1765 he wrote, "The situation of trade with us is at present very dull," and he could not remit owing to the "sudden stagnation of business amongst us." He speaks of the many debts due him, some of which were "unsafe." In 1768, David and John Barclay refused to open business with him, because they had too many connections with Philadelphia and had been disappointed in their remittances. "That determines us at present not to open any new accounts at

---

[1] Freeman & Osland wrote April 28, 1763, saying that "the failure of remittances from America rendered it impossible for them to fill his orders." Collins wrote to Neate, Pigon & Booth, "I shall be very cautious of ordering any more Goods than I can pay for to your satisfaction" (April 30, 1767).

[2] He made a strenuous effort to collect money. Patrick Riley, Bound Brook, September 21, 1763, wrote, "I rec[d] thine of the 8[mo] 4, 1763, which Required in the most strickest manner thy money." John Goldy, New Mills, March 6, 1764, "As an Acknowledgement for thy Extrornery favor and patience in Waiting so long for thy Money," etc.

least with such only whose Capitals will enable them to preserve
that punctuality we used formerly to experience from our old Friends
in your City and is absolutely necessary to render a connection ac-
ceptable; so confident we are that we will venture to assert under
the late and indeed present state of your Trade, it is not in the power
of any man with a slender Capital to give that satisfaction to his
correspondents either he could wish or they expect." Even in 1769,
Collins could write, "The great difficulty we labour under either in
selling goods for cash at any profit or in collecting it where it has
been long overdue." He had succeeded in reducing his debt to
Hyde and Hamilton to £167 in 1767, but he did not clear himself
of his indebtedness to Neate till 1771, when the account current
rendered in December showed a balance in Collins's favor of £514,
and in consequence Neate sent him a hamper of porter and a North
Wiltshire cheese.[1]

While in individual cases and in certain sections such as Charles
Town [2] and parts of the West Indies, the balance of trade was against

---

[1] The account between William Allason of Falmouth, Virginia, and his brother
in Glasgow ran as follows:

December 1760	Debit	£2129	Balance	1342
" 1762	"	1342	"	1392[a]
" 1763	"	1657[b]	"	1258
" 1764	"	1595[b]	"	904
" 1765	"	1021[b]	"	603
" 1766	"	1048[b]	"	697
" 1767	"	717[b]	"	362
" 1768	"	388[c]	"	182

[a] Including £50 interest with no credit allowance.
[b] Principal and interest.
[c] Principal and interest and postage.

The letters from Henry Cruger to Aaron Lopez of Newport, Rhode Island,
show a similar situation. In March, 1768, the indebtedness of Lopez to Cruger
was £11,000 stg, with a prospect of a reduction to £9000. In 1767 it was £10,514
(Commerce of Rhode Island, i. 189, 229).

[2] The Charles Town merchants generally had balances to their credit in England, so that the drain of specie in that direction was trifling as compared with the
North. But there was a drain of specie northward, because of the large amounts
of potatoes, onions, flour, and other staples imported from the northern colonies,
for which there was only a little rice to give in return. Few provisions were raised
on the plantations of South Carolina, and no Irish potatoes for export till 1768
(South Carolina Gazette, June 27, 1768). It was estimated in 1770, that specie was
drawn from the colony in three ways: (1) by the payment of the king's duties
in silver; (2) by the trade with the northern colonies, "who take a very incon-

England, in the region from North Carolina northward it was in England's favor during the eighteenth century with the single exception of the period from 1774 to 1777. Imports and exports approached most nearly an equilibrium during the non-importation period, the year 1769 especially, when the balance was only slightly in England's favor. At all other times the imports largely exceeded the exports, though the volume of excess varied during our period from £200,000 in 1769 to £4,000,000 in 1771, with a mean of about £800,000.[1] This meant that a debt existed to the English merchants which American merchants and planters were trying to pay off as rapidly as they could. But when trade was dull, times hard, markets bad, prices low and falling, stocks glutted, and money scarce, the merchants in England and Scotland suffered no less than did those in America. The merchants' letters to their American correspondents, already quoted, show their apprehensions. Others are to the same effect. "Never was such times here before," wrote Jeremiah Osborn of London to Aaron Lopez in 1767; Henry Cruger, writing in the same year from Bristol, spoke of the "close Dunning from necessitous Manufacturers and Tradesmen" to which he was subjected, and said that nothing but "a great share of Natural Fortitude of Mind" kept him "from sinking under [his] present Calamities." The situation in Scotland was worse even than in England. "People of the best credit cannot borrow a shilling. The Glasgow and Edinburgh banks lending none and calling in all their credits, offering by public advertisements 5 pct for any sums at any time," wrote Robert Allason, in 1763, when he was in great distress for money. "Public credits are bad, stocks lower than ever known before. London exchange 3 pct against us, and a general stagnation of payments here, so that I never remember things in a worse situation." If bills of exchange, he writes again, are not sent "they wont find a man

siderable quantity of our produce in payment for their goods;" (3) by sea voyages to the same colonies for health, pleasure, change of air, or education. Thirty-two people are mentioned as going in that year to Rhode Island, Philadelphia, New York, or Boston, and taking with them 3500 guineas, chiefly in half joes and dollars. See an interesting letter in the Georgia Gazette on this subject, October 18, 1764.

[1] "Oil without Vinegar and Dignity without Pride, or British, American, and West India Interests Considered, Together with a Chart showing the Rise and Fall of the Trade between the Two Countries, By Macall Medford," 2d edition, London, 1807.

in Britain that will lend them £500 cash on their joint credit. I never knew such times. Trade is still very bad, credit quite at a stand. In short this country was never in such a situation and if things dont mend soon there must be a general bankruptcy" (1764).

Thus it is evident that during the first half of the decade trade conditions in England, Scotland, and America were unsatisfactory and growing worse. The grievances of the Boston merchants outlined with unusual fulness the opinions generally held by merchants and expressed more or less fully in their letters. But while specific grievances affected each section and seaport differently, the one great grievance that seemed to affect all alike was the scarcity of hard money. While local debts could be paid in kind or in paper currency, British balances had to be met in johannes, moiodores, pistoles, dollars, and pistareens, according to their value as sterling. The royal revenues had to be met in the same manner. It did not make any difference to the man who paid these duties that they might not in all cases be sent to England to be receipted for at the Exchequer. He had to pay them in any case, and if the amounts received were spent or might be spent in America, the whole eventually found its way across the water to meet trade balances. Whatever may be the actual facts in the case, the colonists believed that their hard money was being drawn off to England.[1] Even as early as 1763, Van Cortlandt could write from New York, "Nothing is at present in so grate demand as cash, the London ships have carried off the gratest part of our silver and gold."

If this was the case before 1764, it was much more true after that date, when the collections, as entered in the Receiver General's accounts,[2] show large increases, when the West Indian trade, which

---

[1] This subject will bear further investigation. The author of American Husbandry deems it a "hackneyed argument" to say that the money of the northern colonies was "laid out in merchandize with Britain" (ii. 242). But the colonists believed profoundly that it was so. Samuel Adams said, "The Dutys upon the goods imported from [England] and consumed here, together with those which are laid upon almost every Branch of our Trade all of which center in dry Cash in her Coffers amounts to a very great sum" (Writings, i. 42–43, 62, 114).

[2] The following is taken from the Annual Abstracts of the Receiver General, 1746–1780 (Public Record Office, Treasury 38:357):

1762	Plantation duty	£721
1763	" "	1326
1764	" "	1031

brought in much hard money, was rigidly controlled, and when
smuggling was reduced almost to a standstill.[1] The Stamp Act
congress sounded a note of warning when it declared that the scarcity
of specie rendered the payment of "the duties imposed by several
late acts of parliament absolutely impracticable." The warning
was hardly needed, for the danger was in every one's mind. The
town of Roxbury said in 1769, that instead of being reconciled to
the revenue acts, "thro' length of time which hath a tendency to
wear off the gloom of difficulties, we daily find them more and more
burdensome; and when we view the trade and commerce of the province under a very sensible decay and loaded with embarrassments,
and the little circulating cash which we have left daily draining from
us and the revenue officers like the horse leech cry, Give, Give, our
groans and complaints are increased."[2] Salem reported that 7000
ounces of silver had been collected from the Townshend duties on
goods "brought to town for exportation or consumption," thus im-
poverishing provinces "to maintain swarms of useless officers in luxury
and extravagance;"[3] and one enterprising writer estimated in 1768

1765	Plantation duty	£2959
1766	" "	7378
1767	Plantation duty	3910
	By 4 George III	29,685
	" 6 George II	10
	" 6 George III	272
	Fines and Forfeitures	684
1768	Plantation duty	517
	By 4 George III	14,802
	" 6 George III	8765
	" 7 George III	86
	Fines and Forfeitures	119
1769	Plantation duty	1075
	By 6 George II	75
	" 4 George III	6047
	" 6 George III	2655
	" 7 George III	708
	Fines and Forfeitures	1217
	Seizures by Ships of War (per 4 George III, c. 15) .	597

[1] See the grievances of the Boston merchants, p. 169 and note 1, above.
Even in 1763, Van Cortlandt could say, "Here [New York] the men of warr and
customs officials search every vessel and have seized several," "Several vessels
have been seized this week past, therefore be careful of contraband goods."

[2] Boston Gazette, May 22, 1769.

[3] Pennsylvania Chronicle, July 18, 1769.

that the silver already drawn from the province "if beat into plates would entirely cover the road to the Borders of York government," but that the sum, large as it was, "would not in any ways equal the amount lost to the province by the destruction of its trade." [1]

IV

Such a situation as this called for drastic remedies. The popular solution of the difficult problem was frugality and thrift in daily life, the refusal to purchase certain articles that could be obtained only by importation from abroad, the manufacture of such necessities as might be made in America, and the finding of substitutes in cases where articles or commodities could not be duplicated. The movement against extravagance in dress and lavishness and display at funerals had begun early in the decade, but the first certain hint of a non-consumption policy, as a reply to the British revenue measures, was given early in November, 1764, in a letter to Jasper Mauduit in England, in which the writer or writers asserted that as their trade would be greatly cramped by the scarcity of money, necessity would oblige them to do without such luxuries as cambric, lawn, calico, and other foreign imports, and Spanish and Portuguese wines.[2]

But no definite step appears to have been taken until after the passage of the Townshend Act was known in America, when on October 28, 1767, a large number of the people of Boston came together in town meeting and having presented in vigorous language

---

[1] Boston Gazette, July 11, 1768.

[2] This letter is not signed and there is no clue to its authorship. Its content is similar to the first part of that sent by Otis, Cushing, Gray, Adams, and Sheafe to Dennys De Berdt in December, 1765 (Massachusetts Papers, pp. 6–7), but it differs from the latter in containing the non-consumption clause and omitting the constitutional arguments that occupy so large a space in the latter document. As it was also sent to Richard Jackson in the spring of 1766, after the Otis letter had been sent to De Berdt and as the merchants at this time paid little attention to the constitutional claim, it is possible that the Society had something to do with it, particularly as Otis, Cushing, and Gray were all members of the Merchants' Club (Rowe's Diary, manuscript, December 14, 20, 24, 31, January 9, 10, 11, 1764–1765). This letter is not included in the printed Massachusetts Papers, but will be found in the manuscript collection.

Drake mentions a non-importation and non-consumption agreement of August, 1764 (History and Antiquities of Boston, p. 679), but I have been entirely unable to find contemporary evidence for it. It is certain that no non-importation agreement was made at that time, and had a non-consumption agreement been entered into in any formal way, it would surely be recorded in the newspapers.

a statement of existing evils — heavy indebtedness, burdensome taxation, a declining trade suffering under great embarrassments and heavy impositions, scarcity of money, and an unfavorable balance of trade — entered into a formal self-denying agreement not to purchase, after December 31st, some forty articles of luxury or superfluity — silks, diamonds, furs, and millinery — and sundry commodities — glue, starch, cheese, etc. — that were probably deemed capable of production in America. At the same time the meeting put itself on record against importation and in favor of manufacturing, particularly of glass and paper, and warmly advocated the cultivation of a spirit of frugality, hoping thereby to find "a more promising prospect of emerging from the present alarming situation." [1] On the 30th a committee which had been named at the meeting met and began to arrange for subscriptions to the agreement, the form of which had already been prepared. In the meantime the selectmen despatched a letter to other towns in Massachusetts and the near-by provinces, with a copy of the Boston agreement. Providence, following the lead of Boston in all details, adopted the resolves in town meeting on December 2d,[2] and Newport did the same on November 26th. Roxbury [3] passed a similar resolution on December 7th.

The frugality cry was taken up by other towns, was carried northward to Maine and southward to Plymouth and the Cape, was heard in Connecticut, where Windham and Norwich were the first towns to respond, and, as the news spread by the gazettes travelled further south, found welcome in New York, New Jersey, and Pennsylvania, and approval in the remoter bounds of Charles Town and Savannah.[4] "Save your money and you can save your country"

---

[1] Boston Record Commissioners' Reports, xvi. 221–224; Boston Gazette November 2, 1767. This meeting did not adopt a non-importation resolution as is frequently stated.

[2] The town meeting met on November 25, and appointed a committee, which reported on December 2, at which time the resolution was adopted (Providence Town Records, November 25, December 2, 1767; Providence Gazette, December 12, 1767; Massachusetts Historical Society, Broadsides, December 9, 1767).

[3] Memorial History of Boston, ii. 338.

[4] The following towns may be listed, but the number could be greatly increased. Falmouth, Scarborough, Pepperellborough, Biddeford, Wells, Kittery, Old York, Arundel, Newburyport, Billerica, Medfield, Abington, Wellsboro, Ashburnham, Salem, Lexington, Grafton, Dartmouth, Plymouth, Sandwich,

expressed in simple form this self-denying purpose, a purpose that found a place in the daily life of every individual and acted somewhat after the fashion of a body of sumptuary laws. To practise abstention and so to decrease the demand for European goods was within the range even of the humblest, and to lay off ribbons, laces, velvets, silks, and other forms of expensive dress became the first object of the new movement. To wear colonial-made clothing, native homespun, was the inevitable corollary, and everywhere gave added zest to household spinning and weaving. The ladies, young and old, became the sponsors of the new fashion, they donned clothing of their own manufacture, held spinning and weaving parties, and vied with each other, as town competed with town, to make a record of skeins spun and yards produced. From sunrise to sunset, out-of-doors in fair weather and indoors in stormy, spinning bees[1] became the centres of social activity, and in Massachusetts premiums were offered for the best pieces of cloth, serge, sagathy, and shalloon woven in the colony.[2] The men responded less enthusiastically to the new demand and took less kindly to this curtailment of their habits of dress and their social and sporting pleasures. Homespun was neither becoming nor fashionable, and the pleasures of the table, the tavern, and the race-course were not easily resigned, especially in the South.[3] In some quarters the ladies endeavored to make the

---

Truro. For Connecticut towns, see Larned, History of Windham County, ii. 118. The proceedings in Boston and the northern colonies were printed with approval in both the South Carolina and Georgia Gazettes, but I cannot find that any formal action was taken. New Jersey sent Massachusetts her congratulations on the economy resolutions, and Virginia, April 5, 1768, said she was anxiously expecting that some resolves of frugality and industry would be entered into by the merchants of Philadelphia, as the influence of so large a place would be extensive and the lesser towns would be ambitious to follow her example (Boston Gazette, May 9, 1768). All of the non-importation agreements contain non-consumption clauses.

[1] On September 21, 1769, there was held at Taunton "a Spinning Match: (or what is call'd in the Country a Bee)" (Boston Gazette, October 16, 1769).

[2] Boston Gazette, November 2, 1767, October 16, 1769; New London Gazette, April 25, 1766.

[3] One newspaper querist desired to know whether it would not be more probable that "we should soon have more profitable times among us, if the gentlemen's oeconomy or prudence were half equal to that of the ladies" (Boston Gazette, June 6, 1768); and a lady wrote to the South Carolina Gazette upbraiding the men for lack of self-denial, going to club or tavern, gaming, horse-racing, and cock-fighting (October 5, 1769). The South Carolina maidens were not satisfied with

spinning parties as agreeable as possible to the men, by adding dancing and other festivities to the closing routine of the day, but elsewhere such frivolity was frowned upon and prayer and singing terminated the performance.[1] The pleasure of these and other occasions must have been somewhat tempered by the substitution of Hyperion tea for the customary Hyson and Bohea, and by the use of burnt barley, or small field peas, burnt carefully with butter and ground, which were extolled as equal to the best West India coffee.[2]

The many manifestations of the new temper of the colonists met with high popular approval and were widely commented on in the press. At a wedding in Windham the ladies dressed chiefly in clothes of their own making and drank Labrador tea.[3] A citizen of Newport declared that he would not vote for any of the candidates at a coming election who did not appear principally clothed in cloth made either in Rhode Island or in some part of America, and one of the clauses of the Newport agreement of October 30, 1769, was to the same effect.[4] The tailors of the same town had a meeting and offered to work fourpence cheaper on the manufactures of America than on those of other countries and to exact twenty-five per cent more in

a change of clothes, they wanted a change of habits also. New London recommended abstention from the use of spirituous liquors (Boston Gazette, February 1, 1768).

[1] At Gloucester the spinning was followed by the singing of an anthem (Essex Gazette, December 27, 1768).

[2] Hyperion or Labrador tea was a decoction of the leaves of the common "red root" and is described as "something like wild rosemary," with a "very physical taste, of a deep brown color, and generally disliked by those who taste it." It was afterwards advertised as "very wholesome and good for the rheumatism, spleen, and many other disorders and pains." A writer of New Bern, North Carolina, June 10, 1768, noting that Hyperion tea was used in the North "as a succedaneum to that most pernicious and destructive plant Bohea, which annually drains America of thousands," recommended to the people of North Carolina, "with due deference to the refined taste of the ladies, the use of Yeopann Tea." "This plant," the writer adds, "is much used among the lower sort, is of great efficacy, when taken physically, being a powerful sudorific; is no exotic but a domestic of almost every sandy plantation in this province. We hope, therefore, soon to have the pleasure of informing the public that at a meeting of the ladies on such and such a day at such a place, such a number of threads were spun, after which they regaled with Yeopann Tea" (New Hampshire Gazette, July 22, 1768). The yapon (yopon) shrub and "tea" are well known in the South.

[3] Larned, Windham County, ii. 117; Caulkins, History of Norwich, p. 367.

[4] Newport Mercury, February 13, 1769; South Carolina Gazette, November 23, 1769.

making up velvet, silk, and broadcloth, costing over ten shillings a yard.[1] In Massachusetts, members of the Council and the House of Representatives, and the clergy generally, promised to wear cloth and shoes [2] of their own manufacture,[3] and the senior classes at Harvard, Yale, and the College of Rhode Island, now Brown University, appeared in homespun on the occasion of their graduation.[4] Harvard students, on October 24, 1768, resolved not to use tea, and the people of the towns around entered into the same resolution, while here and there, by formal vote, a town would declare a similar intention.[5] The reaction against excessive extravagance at

[1] Newport Mercury, January 30, 1768.

[2] The making of shoes at Lynn had been a New England industry for some years and was now considerably increased to relieve the people of buying the poorer varieties of shoes from England. The better varieties, such as callamanco shoes, the uppers of which were covered with a flowered or striped cloth imported from Flanders, were not made in America at this time. Cheap shoes in the South were made for sale by negro shoemakers on the plantations, and the business brought in considerable revenue to the slave owners. Lynn shoes were exported to Philadelphia and elsewhere.

[3] Boston Gazette, January 4, 1768.

[4] At Brown, the president also wore homespun (John Carter Brown Library, Broadside). The senior class at Yale announced their decision early "that their parents and friends [might] have sufficient time to be providing homespun cloaths for them that none of them [might] be obliged to the hard necessity of unfashionable singularity by wearing imported cloth" (New Hampshire Gazette, January 20, 1767). Madison wrote to his father from Nassau Hall (Princeton) that all the 115 students in the college and the 22 in the grammar school were wearing American cloth, July 23, 1770 (Writings, 1900, i. 7). For extracts from the Harvard "College Books," referring to the wearing of homespun, see our Publications, xviii. 351–352.

[5] Boston Gazette, March 27, 1767. How widespread the actual abstention from the use of British goods and tea-drinking was at this time it is difficult to say. The writer of the Journal of Occurrences, reprinted in the New London Gazette, January 6, 1769, said that the disuse of tea was universal and that retailers reported a falling off in its sale of four fifths; that many towns had entered into formal agreements to stop consumption; and that applications had been made from Georgia and another province for some articles of American manufacture. There was none, he added, available for export, but he knew that the manufacture of linen, cotton, and woollen had greatly increased since the Stamp Act, that almost every house was a manufactory, and that some towns had more looms than houses. So zealous was the spirit, he continued, and so helpful the new artisans brought over that already the country people everywhere were clothing themselves, and in time New England would have a surplus. Probably one must read such statements cautiously. The newspaper writers were very sanguine and often overstated their case, when it came to the expression of a hope or an expectation. As to this particular correspondent, we may well heed Thomas Hutchin-

funerals,[1] in dress, carriages, and rings and gloves to the mourners, had long been under way in the North, and now spread to the South, and the people of Charles Town began to clothe themselves in their own manufactures, reducing the "enormous expense of funerals," therein following "the patriotic example lately set by Christ. Gadsden, Esq., when he buried the best of wives," until it seemed according to a local opinion that black at funerals would be "only worn by the fashionable gentry of the Ethiopian race." [2] In order not to diminish

son's criticism in his letter to Israel Williams, "Nine tenths of what you read of the Journal of Occurrences in Boston is either absolutely false or grossly misrepresented" (Williams Papers, Massachusetts Historical Society, January 26, 1769). There was plenty of tea-drinking in Salem in 1769–1770: see the Holyoke Diaries, 1709–1856.

Patriotic zeal and a proneness to exaggeration must be reckoned with in all these accounts. Lancaster in 1770 was reported to have manufactured 30,000 yards of linen and woollen homespun, and to have in town 50 looms and 700 spinning wheels. Elizabeth went a step further and reported 100,000 yards spun and woven. Yet Gov. Franklin said in 1768 that there was no great increase in the raising of sheep in New Jersey and that there was not wool enough to provide each family with stockings (Pennsylvania Gazette, July 5, 1770; New Jersey Archives, x. 30–31).

There was a noteworthy effort at this time to bring skilled workmen from abroad, and efforts in that direction were successfully made. Wages were higher in the colonies than in England and complaints of artisans leaving England for America were not infrequent. Providence advertised in 1768 for "tradesmen in the mechanick arts," and Boston in 1769 mentioned several persons "lately arrived from abroad" (Providence Gazette, February 13, 1768; Staples, Annals of Providence, pp. 217–218; Boston Record Commissioners' Reports, xvi. 275. Cf. Boston Chronicle, February 13, 1769, for English complaints).

[1] Boston continued to have elaborate funerals, as in the case of Jeremiah Gridley, 1767, when the parade and show were not at all to Rowe's liking. The most costly funeral that Boston ever had was probably that of Andrew Faneuil in 1738, though that of Gov. Leverett in 1680 was certainly the most unique. (Memoir biographical and genealogical of Sir John Leverett, Knt., Governor of Massachusetts, Boston, 1856.)

[2] South Carolina Gazette, March 2, 1769: "Our greatest friend to homespun cloth, Christ. Gadsden, Esq., buried his wife yesterday morning. The town was searched throughout for some of that manufactory to follow as a mourner, but none could be bought and he was obliged to follow in blue cloth. The whole expence of the funeral of the manufacture of England did not amount to more than £3.10 our currency" (equal to 10 sh. sterling). The funeral of Lord Botetourt at Williamsburg in Virginia, 1770, though not as grand as that of Lovelace in New York a century before, showed little restraint in matters of expense. The coffin had eight silver handles and sixteen escutcheons; thirty-two escutcheons ornamented the hearse and the church, where the reading desk, pulpit, and communion table were hung with superfine cloth. There were twenty-eight streamers

the number of sheep and so to lessen the woollen manufacture, towns, fire companies, and individuals, here and there, took solemn counsel to eat no more lamb or mutton during the year.[1]

Perhaps the only article upon which an import duty was imposed by the Townshend Act, that was deemed indispensable to the colonists, was paper, and during the years from 1767 to 1770, when the duty was removed, the manufacture of paper was a matter of great concern. The call for rags, white and clean, became something of a slogan. Save your rags "if you really love your country" was the way one newspaper put it,[2] while another enumerated abstention from tea, the manufacture of paper, and the "wearing old cloths until they were threadbare"[3] as the cardinal points of the frugality doctrine. Paper of excellent quality was made at Milton, Massachusetts, and was used extensively in the province at this period,[4] but the shortness of the supply rendered strict economy necessary.[5] As rags were always scarce, even under the prevailing disposition to save them, substitutes were suggested, such as tow, which was discarded in the manufacture of flax.

But the promotion of manufactures had a wider purpose to serve than the furtherance of the cause of frugality. It was agreed from Massachusetts to Virginia that a marked increase of manufacturing would bring England to terms,[6] and this belief found expression in

for the horses. The total bill must have been considerably over £500 (Botetourt Accounts, Library of Congress).

[1] Pennsylvania Chronicle, February 13, 1769; Boston Record Commissioners' Reports, xvi. 240, 289.

[2] New London Gazette, December 18, 1767.

[3] New Hampshire Gazette, September 30, 1769.

[4] Boston Gazette, November 23, 1767.

[5] The Harvard College Theses of 1768 have at the bottom of the sheet the words, "In Papyrum Miltoni in Nov-Angliâ confectam" (Massachusetts Historical Society, Broadsides). As early as May 2, 1765, the Boston News-Letter was printed on paper manufactured at Milton. The New Hampshire Gazette, January 6, 1769, appeared in a sheet much reduced in size, and the printers in explaining the fact said that for some time they had been using paper not only made in New England but made of rags collected in Portsmouth. The Maryland Gazette apologized in like manner to its readers (Scharf, History of Maryland, i. 114). One man writing to another said, "My paper is poor but 'tis American made which I hope will give you patience in reading and pleasure in reflection." The making of paper in Connecticut was begun in Norwich in 1766 (Caulkins, History of Norwich, p. 367).

[6] To prevent manufacturing in the colonies was one of the main objects of

the resolutions passed in the town meetings of Boston, Providence, New York, and Philadelphia.[1] At Boston, subscription papers for those who wished to coöperate in establishing specific manufactures were placed in the town clerk's office and received considerable attention. Philadelphia laid stress upon the making of paper, but Boston and New York seem to have interested themselves chiefly in the manufacture of duck and linen, hoping thereby to accomplish the double purpose of employing the poorer classes, in distress because of the money stringency, and of arousing England's fears lest the northern colonies should become a centre of manufactures in competition with the mother country. The Boston undertaking was a matter of great interest to the Merchants' Society, and its execution was entrusted to a committee of its members. This committee raised funds, erected buildings, set certain of the poor at work, and calculated very carefully the profit and loss of the enterprise. But how long the effort was continued or whether it was a success or not, I am unable to say.[2]

V

The idea of non-importation of goods from England, as a measure not of economy but of retaliation and boycott, for the express purpose of enforcing a redress of grievances, must have been in the minds of the merchants of America for some time before the plan was finally adopted. It followed the rejection by the House of Commons of the various petitions sent over against the Stamp Act, and was due, as we are told, to the belief that after such rejections the colonists had "nothing to hope for but from themselves."[3] The idea took shape first in New York in October, 1765, apparently among the merchants, who on the 31st of that month gathered in

British policy. "Nothing, certainly would create greater heart burning and discontent in Great Britain than her colonies going into manufactures" (An Essay on Trade and Commerce. . . . Together with Some interesting Reflections on the Importance of our Trade to America. [By J. Cunningham.] London, 1770, p. 197).

[1] Boston Gazette, November 9, 16, 23, 30, 1767; Providence Gazette, December 12, 1767.

[2] Massachusetts Historical Society, O2517, nos. 36, 50, 51 (canvas), 73, 74, 80–95 (linen); Boston Record Commissioners' Reports, xvi. 222, 226–227, 230–232, 239, 240–250, 275 (condition of the poor), xviii. 71, 73. For New York, cf. Becker, op. cit., p. 71.

[3] 6 Massachusetts Historical Collections, ix. 243.

the Long Room of George Burn's tavern, the old house of James De Lancey, and there passed resolutions constituting the first non-importation agreement in America. The merchants engaged that none of them should order any goods from England till the Stamp Act was repealed, that the orders already sent out, and not executed, should be countermanded, with certain exceptions, and that they would accept no goods on commission or assist in the sale of any sent there. This agreement was signed by two hundred merchants, while the retailers, a few days afterwards, promised "not to buy any goods, wares or merchandize of any person or persons whatsoever, that shall be shipped from Great Britain after the first day of January next, unless the Stamp Act shall be repealed." [1] The Albany merchants, always influenced by the policy of their New York brethren, entered into a similar agreement in January, 1766.[2]

The merchants of Philadelphia, "in imitation of the noble example of New York," gathered together, in November, 1765, and to the number of three hundred and seventy signed a memorial and entered into a non-importation agreement. The memorial laid stress on the drain of specie, due to the balance of trade, which was heavily against Pennsylvania, even under the most favorable conditions. The terms of the agreement were these: (1) To instruct their correspondents in England not to ship goods until the Stamp Act was repealed; (2) to countermand all orders for goods, except in the case of such merchants as were owners of vessels already gone or clearing for Great Britain, who were at liberty to bring back in them coals, casks of earthenware, grindstones, pipes, iron pots, empty bottles, and such other bulky articles as owners were accustomed to load as ballast, but no dry goods of any kind, except such dyestuffs and utensils as were necessary for carrying on manufactures; (3) to continue non-importation until May 1, 1766.[3]

---

[1] Boston Gazette, November 11, 18, 1765; New York Colonial Documents, vii. 800; Becker, op. cit., p. 30.

[2] New York Gazette and Weekly Mercury, January 27, 1766.

[3] Boston Gazette, November 25, 1765; Massachusetts Papers (Massachusetts Historical Society). This document is not in the printed collection. The committee appointed to see that this agreement was carried out consisted of Thomas Willing, Samuel Mifflin, Thomas Montgomery, Samuel Howell, Samuel Wharton, John Rhea, William Fisher, Joshua Fisher, Peter Chevalier, Benjamin Fuller, and Abel James.

Of the three leading seaports, Boston was the last to act. On November 25th the Boston Gazette hoped that Philadelphia's example would be followed by the merchants of this and other American ports, and appealed to householders generally to refuse to buy English goods, "even though it should be to the ruin of a few private and selfish men." Once a beginning were made, it said, the spirit would "ketch from town to town and province to province, than which nothing can more contribute to a speedy redress of our grievances." The Boston merchants were quick to respond. On November 30th the call for a meeting was sent out to be held on December 3d, in the afternoon, at the British Coffee House, and there an agreement was adopted, which was renewed and recast in more formal fashion on the 9th, and signed by over two hundred merchants. The terms were substantially the same as those of Philadelphia, except in the list of exemptions, which included hemp, canvas, salt, coals, grindstones, pipes, empty bottles, wool-cards, brimstone, copperas, dyeing stuffs, utensils for carrying on manufactures, and such articles as might be absolutely necessary for carrying on the fishery. The resolves were to be binding on all subscribers, as soon as two hundred of those who were engaged in trade in Massachusetts had signed it, and was to last until May 5, 1766. By December 16th the required number had been obtained, and the news was brought to Boston that the merchants and traders of both Salem and Marblehead had "unanimously come into the same resolve." [1] The combined action of the three leading cities had the desired effect. Through the efforts of the British merchants, who spared no pains to accomplish the result, the Stamp Act was repealed. The first effort at non-importation was successful because the merchants on

[1] Boston Gazette, December 2, 9, 16, 1765. The credit of originating the plan of non-importation has been given to Samuel Adams, but even if we could believe that one man, and he not a merchant, could have conceived the idea, the evidence is not sufficient to warrant the assertion. There is nothing whatever in Adams's writings to show that non-importation was in his mind at this time. The sentence printed in Wells, Life of Adams, i. 80–82, at best refers to non-consumption and not to non-importation, and probably was not written by Adams at all. Cushing does not include the instruction in which the sentence occurs in his edition of Adams's Writings. It is not until the merchants had had their meeting of March 1, 1768, that Adams comes out with a statement which might possibly be construed as referring to non-importation. The plan, by whomsoever broached, did not have its rise in Boston.

both sides of the water confined their statements of grievances to matters of trade and finance.

But an opportunity for a second and more noteworthy experiment soon came. On June 29, 1767, the Townshend Act, which levied a duty on glass, lead, painters' colors, tea, and paper, became a law, to go into effect the 20th of November following. The non-consumption campaign was in full vigor and the merchants, deeming the new imposts less injurious to trade than the other burdens and restrictions, at first confined their non-importing activities to articles of luxury, under the agreement of October 28, 1767.[1] But the events of the winter of 1767–1768 and the manner in which the American Board of Customs Commissioners put the act into execution must have influenced the merchants to revive the expedient of 1765 and to adopt again the plan of stopping, under certain limitations, the importing of goods from Great Britain. On March 1, 1768, a meeting of the Body, made up of ninety-eight merchants, was held at the British Coffee House, and with William Phillips as moderator voted to try again the non-importation plan. The Body chose a committee, of which John Rowe was chairman and Edward Payne secretary. This committee met on the 3d and again in an all-day session on the 4th and framed the articles of the agreement. The report was unanimously approved at the meeting of the Body on the evening of the 4th, and, among others, the following articles were adopted:

Voted, That we will not for one year send for any European Commodities Excepting Salt, Coals, Fish hooks and lines, Hemp and Duck, Barr-lead and Shott, Wool-cards and Card-wire.

Voted, That in the purchase of such articles as we shall stand in need of we will give a constant preference to such Persons as shall subscribe to these Resolutions.

Voted, That we will in our separate capacities inform our several Correspondents of the Reasons and point out to them the Necessity of withholding our usual order for their Manufactures, to the end that the said Impediments may be removed and Trade and Commerce may again flourish.

Voted, That these Votes and Resolutions be obligatory or binding

---

[1] James Bowdoin as a subscriber to the agreement refused to import a set of Boydell's engravings (6 Massachusetts Historical Collections, ix. 84–85).

on us from and after the time that these or other similar or tending to the same salutary purpose be adopted by most of the principal trading Towns in this and the neighboring colonies.[1]

In obtaining subscriptions to this agreement, certain questions arose which were dealt with at an adjourned meeting on the 9th, when it was voted that subscribers were "bound not to forward their orders for any goods till the first Tuesday in May" (1768), in order that the "determination of the merchants and traders in the neighbouring Towns and Colonies" might be known, and a committee was appointed, John Hancock, chairman, John Rowe, Edward Payne, William Phillips, Melatiah Bourne, Henderson Inches, and John Erving, Jr., "to correspond with the Merchants in the other Trading Towns and Provinces." Letters were sent out on the 16th by this committee to points as far south as Charles Town, urging the merchants to coöperate in the non-importation movement, on the ground that a refusal to import goods would procure relief and be of more service than any remonstrance.[2] In response to this letter, the Providence merchants met on the 17th and adopted the agreement. Two weeks later the merchants of New York began a series of meetings, at one of which, held at Bolton and Sigel's tavern on April 8th, was established the New York Chamber of Commerce,[3] composed of twenty-four merchants, organized for the purpose of "encouraging commerce, supporting industry, adjusting disputes relative to trade and navigation, and procuring such laws and regulations as [might] be found necessary for the benefit of trade in general." A week later, acting on the report of a committee appointed to obtain the general sentiment of the merchants, importers, and retailers, a non-importation agreement was entered upon, constituting a voluntary engagement to each other that they would not "sell on their own accounts or on commission, nor buy or sell for any per-

---

[1] As illustrating the interest taken in the non-importation situation, attention may be called to the appearance of the following subject among the Quaestiones, announced for debate at the coming Commencement of Harvard College, in July, 1768:

IX. An contractus mercatorii, ad perniciem publicam tendentes, obligant.

[2] Massachusetts Papers (MS.), no. 87. This document is printed, not quite accurately, in Massachusetts Papers, p. 58. Also see Rowe's Diary, under dates given.

[3] Memorial History of New York, iv. 516.

44

son whomsoever any goods [save a very few enumerated articles] which shall be shipped from Great Britain after October 1, 1768, until the acts are repealed," providing Boston and Philadelphia adopted similar measures by June 1st, following.[1]

Letters were immediately sent to the merchants of Philadelphia and Boston, and on the 25th the former, with the letters of both Boston and New York before them, met at "The Lodge," and after listening to an address on the grievances of the colony [2] took into consideration the question of non-importation. No decision was reached at this meeting, and during July the merchants continued to meet and to consider a number of objections, chief among which was the fear lest non-importation according to the New York plan should "serve to create a monopoly by enabling the merchants with capital to lay in a large stock of the proscribed commodities before the agreement became effective." [3] Boston on the other hand

---

[1] New York Gazette and the Weekly Mercury, April 18, 1768.

[2] "Gentlemen: You are called together to consider what answer shall be returned to the Brethren of Boston and New York, who desire to know whether we will unite with them in stopping the importation of goods from Great Britain until certain acts are repealed."
The speaker then recounted the special grievances of Pennsylvania:
1. The law against steel and steel furnaces.
2. The law against plating and slitting mills.
3. The law against carrying wool freely from one colony to another.
4. The prohibition against sending logwood to foreign markets.
5. The obligation to carry Portuguese and Spanish wines to England.
6. The duty on Madeira wines.
7. The emptying of British jails upon the province.
8. The restrictions upon the fisheries and the duties on foreign molasses and sugars.
9. The necessity of supplying themselves with goods through England at 20 per cent and even 40 per cent increase.
10. The Stamp Act, Declaratory Act, and Townshend Act (Massachusetts Historical Society, Broadsides).

[3] Becker, op. cit., p. 62. The Pennsylvania Chronicle, July 23, 1768, contains a list of fourteen queries proposed to the committee of the Philadelphia merchants, "now sitting," for consideration, each raising the question as to the wisdom of the New York agreement. The writer asks "Whether precipitate combination, at the time of great distress in England, to import no British manufactures would not be a means of irritating and making enemies of the inhabitants of Great Britain at the same time distressing ourselves." The writer urges patience and reasonableness, manufacturing and getting on without the taxed goods, and says that what may be prudent in the eastern governments (New York and New Eng-

acted at once. On May 2, 1768, the whole Body met in the Representatives Room in the Town House, and there accepted the resolutions of New York, binding themselves not to write for any goods after June 1st nor to import any after October 1st, until the Townshend duties were removed. On the same day Gloucester, probably acting on the Boston letter of March 16th, promised to stop importation for a year from the date of the meeting.[1]

Hillsborough's circular letter of April 21, 1768, to the governors of all the colonies in America, roused a great deal of resentment among the colonists. It was called out by the general letter issued on February 11th by the speaker of the Massachusetts House of Representatives, and was addressed to the speaker of the assembly of each colony upon the continent of North America, and characterized that letter as "of a most dangerous and factious tendency calculated to inflame the minds of the king's subjects in America." Such an interpretation was rightly deemed unjust and absurd. Hillsborough's further demand that the governors persuade their assemblies to ignore the letter and to treat it "with the contempt it deserved" created in the colonists a deeper sense of their common interest and so furthered the cause of non-importation. This ill-advised measure, taken in conjunction with the attempts made in the summer of 1768 to enforce the acts of trade, not only added to the grievances of the importers and merchants generally but strengthened their determination to persist in their work. On July 18th, the Standing Committee, consisting of John Rowe, John Hancock, Edward Payne, Henderson Inches, Melatiah Bourne, and Thomas Boylston, met at the British Coffee House, and on the 25th issued a call for a general meeting at

---

land) may be imprudent in the middle and southern, "seeing we widely differ in many circumstances."

[1] The following is the Gloucester agreement:

"We whose names are underwritten are of opinion that every legal measure for freeing the country from the present embarrassments should be adopted, and among others the stopping the importation of goods from Great Britain. We promise that we will not for one year from the above date [May 2, 1768] write for any goods, except such as are absolutely necessary for the carrying on the Fishery and that we will not take any English goods to sell on commission and we further promise that we will write to our correspondents and desire their interest and influence to put a stop to growing evils of offices that are multiplying among us." Epes Sargent, Nathaniel Allen, Daniel Sargent, Winthrop Sargent, William Ellery, Jr. (Massachusetts Historical Society, O2517, no. 38).

Faneuil Hall, "to consult measures for the better regulation of the trade." The general meeting was postponed until August 1st, but on the 28th the committee drew up the following resolutions:

The Merchants and Traders in the Town of Boston, having taken into consideration the deplorable situation of the Trade and the many difficulties it at present labours under on account of the scarcity of money, which is daily decreasing for want of other remittances to discharge our debts in Great Britain and the large sums collected by the officers of the Customs for duties on goods imported — the heavy taxes levied to discharge the debts contracted by the governments in the late warr — the embarrassments and restrictions laid on the Trade by the several late acts of parliament, together with the bad success of our Cod Fishery this season and the discouraging prospect of the Whale Fishery by which our principal sources of Remittances are like to be greatly diminished, and we thereby rendered unable to pay the debts we owe the Merchants in Great Britain and to continue the importation of goods from thence,

We, the subscribers, in order to relieve the Trade under those discouragements, to promote industry, frugality and oeconomy and to discourage luxury and every kind of extravegance, do promise and engage to and with each other as follows.

That we will not send for or import from Great Britain this Fall, either on our own account or on commission, any other goods than what are already ordered for the Fall supply.

That we will not send for or import any kind of goods or merchandize from Great Britain, either on our own account or on commission or any otherwise, from January 1, 1769, to January 1, 1770, except salt, coals, fishhooks and lines, hemp, duck, bar-lead and shot, wool-cards and card-wire.

That we will not purchase of any factors or others any kind of goods imported from Great Britain, from January 1, 1769, to January 1, 1770.

That we will not import on our own account or on commission or purchase from any who shall import from any other colony in America from January 1, 1769, to January 1, 1770, any tea, glass, paper, or other goods commonly imported from Great Britain.

That we will not from and after January 1, 1769, import into the province any tea, paper, glass, or painters' colours until the acts imposing duties on these articles have been repealed.[1]

These resolutions were presented to the Whole Body when it finally met at Faneuil Hall on August 1, 1768, and were there formally

[1] Massachusetts Historical Society, O2517, no. 71.

adopted, "with greater unanimity than was shown in the time of the Stamp Act."[1] There were present at the meeting, however, but sixty-two merchants, of whom sixty entered their names as subscribers,[2] thus constituting a new body, the Subscribers, within the older group of those who had become members of the Society in 1763, and a very much smaller number than were those who signed the agreement in 1765. Already the old organization was breaking up. Though between August 1st and 8th the number of subscribers was increased, the increase does not appear to have been marked, and it is likely that the meeting of August 8th, at which one hundred were present, was a gathering of those only who had promised to support the movement.[3] The lead of Boston was followed by adjoining towns. Salem, after many meetings held between August 23d and September 6th, finally adopted on the latter date the Boston resolutions without alteration.[4] Other towns did the same, and where formal agreements were wanting resolutions of approval were passed in town meeting.[5]

The New York merchants, acting under the influence of the Boston agreement and hoping to meet the objections of the Philadelphia merchants, now reconsidered the situation, and entered into a new arrangement of a much more detailed and definite character. On August 27, 1768, they subscribed the following resolves:

---

[1] Boston Gazette, August 15, 1768.

[2] Rowe, Diary, August 1, 1768. The proceedings and agreement are given in full in the Boston Chronicle, May 1, 1769, and the agreement is printed in John Mein's pamphlet to be mentioned later.

[3] Rowe, Diary, August 2 and 8, 1768.

[4] The situation in Salem was aggravated by the division in the town between Rescinders and Non Rescinders. Four of the Salem merchants were among the seventeen members of the Massachusetts House of Representatives who voted to rescind the resolutions upon which the letter of February 11th was based, and they had to defend themselves against the attack of their fellow townsmen (Boston Gazette, July 25, August 1, 1768).

[5] As at Norwich: "We give this public testimony of our hearty and unanimous approbation of the resolutions the merchants have entered into to stop the importation of British goods; we will frown upon all who endeavour to frustrate these good designs, and avoid all correspondence with those merchants who shall dare to violate these obligations" (January 29, 1770, Caulkins, History of Norwich, p. 369).

That we will not send for from Great Britain, either upon our own account or on commission, this Fall, any other goods than what we have already ordered.

That we will not import any kind of merchandize from Great Britain, either on our own account or on commission or any otherwise, nor purchase from any factor or others, any kind of goods imported from Great Britain directly or by way of any of the other colonies or by way of the West Indies that shall be shipped from Great Britain after November 1, until the fore-mentioned acts of parliament imposing duties on paper, glass, tea, or painters' colours be repealed, except only coals, salt, sail-cloth, wool-cards and card-wire, grindstones, chalk, lead, tin, sheet-copper, and German steel.

We further agree not to import any kind of merchandize from Hamburgh and Holland directly from thence, nor by any other way whatever, more than what we have already ordered (except tiles and bricks).

We also promise to countermand all orders given for Great Britain, on or since the 16th inst., by the first conveyance, ordering those goods not to be sent unless the fore-mentioned duties are taken off.

And we further agree that if any person or persons, subscribers thereto, shall take any advantage by importing any kind of goods that are herein restricted, directly or indirectly, contrary to the true intent and meaning of this agreement such person or persons shall by us be deemed enemies to this country.

Lastly, we agree that if any goods shall be consigned or sent over to us, contrary to our agreement in this subscription, such goods so imported shall be lodged in some public warehouse, there to be kept under confinement until the fore-mentioned acts are repealed.

This agreement was signed "by nearly all the merchants in town," and several days later, on September 5th, the retailers and tradesmen made a formal promise to support the merchants and to refrain from dealing with such of them as did not adhere to or subscribe the articles adopted on August 27th.[1]

This revised and enlarged agreement of the New York merchants, though showing traces of Boston influence, is a distinct advance in the direction of greater fulness and rigidity. For the first time violators were construed as "enemies of the country," for the first time the requirement was made that goods sent contrary to the agreement should be stored in warehouses until the acts were repealed,

[1] New York Gazette or Weekly Post Boy, September 12, 1768. Printed also in a supplement to the Boston Gazette, September 19, 1768.

and for the first time since 1765 the retail merchants entered formally into the movement. The promise to countermand all orders sent since August 16th and to import no goods from Holland or Hamburg seem designed on the one hand to prevent an accumulation of goods and so to meet the Philadelphia charge of monopoly, on the other to put a stop to smuggling from the European Continent contrary to the Act of 1663.[1] When the news of New York's action reached Boston, it was greeted with manifest approval. At a town meeting held on September 13th, a vote was passed expressing "high satisfaction," [2] and at Providence an agreement was entered into in town meeting on October 24th, similar to that of New York.

Philadelphia had thus far taken no part in the movement, and expressions of contempt because of the "tame disposition" of the Philadelphians began to appear. One New York writer, probably angry at the objections raised by the Philadelphia merchants, wrote:

It is said that it is owing only to a few dry goods merchants that the agreement is not made. It is a most melancholy consideration that only a few inhabitants of one City, contemptible to the last degree for their mercenary principles and abject pusilanimity should be able to obstruct and even disconcert measures so universally applauded. That Merchants of Dry Goods, a business, which though at some times neces-

---

[1] Professor Becker says in commenting on these resolutions: "If the provision making the agreement effective in part from August 16 was designed to meet the charge of monopoly, the provision regarding the Dutch trade was probably designed to prevent, in part at least, the smuggling from Holland. Thus early the two-fold weakness of the non-importation policy was manifest: if sufficiently comprehensive it gave a monopoly to those who inaugurated it; if limited to England, it enriched the smuggler" (op. cit., p. 63). The distinction here made seems to me too precise. There is ample evidence to show that the richer merchants, certainly in Boston and Philadelphia, suffered heavily for their self-denial. Take the case of John Barrett & Sons of Boston, who countermanded their English orders two months before the agreement was signed, and that of the merchants of Philadelphia mentioned in Drinker's letter (Pennsylvania Magazine, xiv. 43) who felt the "present stagnation the most severely." While it may be that the retailers depended on smuggling for their profits, I have seen no sufficient evidence to prove the point, nor does Professor Becker furnish such.

[2] "The Honble Thomas Cushing, Esq. communicated to the Town a Letter lately received from a Committee of Merchants in the City of New York, acquainting him with their Agreement relative to a Non-Importation of British Goods. Whereupon the Town by a Vote expressed their high satisfaction therein" (Boston Record Commissioners' Reports, xvi. 264).

sary, certainly drains the colonies of their specie, more than all other professions put together (even that of the lawyers not excepted) — that this least useful part of the community should be able to do this is humiliating and contemptible and all people and tradesmen should treat them as they deserve.[1]

But Philadelphia was reaching the end of her vacillation. On September 28, 1768, Stephen Collins wrote:

There is some combination at present in agitation respecting non-importing goods on account of the duties, etc, as there is a meeting advertised for that purpose to-morrow, but I rather think they will not succeed in so injudicious a step.[2]

In November, 1768, and again in February, 1769, the Philadelphia merchants drafted and sent memorials to the merchants of England, recounting their grievances and urging intervention in their behalf. In the first memorial, which was based on an earlier draft of November 1, 1765, they confined themselves to trade restrictions, but in the second, which was printed and sent to individual correspondents in all the English cities, they declared the acts of parliament to be unconstitutional and destructive of their rights as British subjects, and they said that unless their trade was speedily relieved from "those unnatural and useless fetters" commerce between Great Britain and the colonies must of necessity greatly diminish and the general importation of goods suddenly cease.[3]

In this memorial of February 6, 1769, the Philadelphia merchants raised for the first time, as far as the merchants were concerned, the constitutional claim, which, though frequently and strongly presented hitherto by individuals, town meetings, and general assemblies, had not as yet been taken up by the traders and importers in their complaints. In so doing the Philadelphians were changing their status as merchants into that of patriots and radicals. It was

---

[1] One is reminded of Pitt's famous characterization of traders and merchants, as "Little, paltry, peddling fellows, venders of two penny wares and falsehoods, who under the idea of trade, sell everything in their power — honour, truth, conscience," etc. In Charles Town, South Carolina, a wholesale dealer was respectable but a retail dealer was not, and even a wholesale or commission merchant must deal in indigo and rice and not in other things.

[2] Collins Papers.

[3] Pennsylvania Journal, February 9, 1769. Printed in full in the Boston Chronicle, February 13, 1769, where it occupies three and a half columns.

a significant change, for just as the resolutions of the New York and Massachusetts assemblies aroused resentment in England, because of the stress laid upon rights and privileges and the so-called illegal and unconstitutional encroachments of crown and parliament, claims which Englishmen could not understand and would not tolerate, so now the appearance of the same argument in the merchants' memorial offended many of their English friends, and chilled the enthusiasm of many of those who had been chiefly responsible for the repeal of the Stamp Act and were in the main sympathetic to the American side of the case, as long as it concerned trade grievances only. The memorial [1] reached England at about the same time as did the petition of the New York assembly [2] of December 17th to the House of Lords and the resolutions of the same body adopted December 31st, the latter of which, we are told, so exasperated the House of Commons that the merchants' plea had no chance of consideration. Many of the British merchants wrote to America that the time was not opportune for energetic action on their part, but that as parliament was probably favorable to a repeal of the Townshend Act, it would be better to wait. They urged upon their friends in America to abstain from violence, apply themselves steadily to the encouragement of frugality and manufactures, adhere to non-importation, and say less about the constitutional issue. The Philadelphia merchants were highly esteemed in England and their relations with their English correspondents are exceedingly instructive, but unfortunately for the hope of a peaceful settlement of the dispute, the advice from England was disregarded, and from this time forward both acts of violence and renewals of the constitutional claims served but to widen the breach.[3]

---

[1] There were four memorials from the merchants of Philadelphia: those of November, 1765; November, 1768; February 6, 1769; and March 10, 1769. The last was sent only to the merchants of London.

[2] The petition of the New York assembly to the House of Lords is printed in the New York Gazette, April 17, 1768, and in the Pennsylvania Journal, April 20, 1768.

[3] "Had a petition come over from your merchants on the principle of inexpediency instead of from your assembly denying the right, the law would ere now have been repealed" (Letter from London, Pennsylvania Chronicle, April 3, 1769). The advice to stick to the non-consumption and non-importation agreements and avoid riots, mobs, and such illegal measures, and lay less stress upon constitutional rights, came from men who were certain to lose by the process and

At the meetings of February 6th and March 10th the Philadelphia merchants finally committed themselves to the cause of non-importation.[1] Though I can give no copy of the final compact, its terms are probably much the same as those of Newcastle County, Delaware, which were adopted on August 28, 1769,[2] and reproduce those of Philadelphia, as did the New Haven terms reproduce those of New York, and the Salem and Gloucester terms those of Boston. The compact, which is deserving of careful study, runs as follows:

We the subscribers, freeholders, and freemen, of the County of New-Castle, upon Deleware, taking into consideration, that our trade is restricted, our rights invaded, arbitrary courts, wholy dependent upon ministers, erected over us, our present security destroyed, by some late acts of the British parliament; and that a plan is laid, and measures adopted in our mother country, which, if carried into execution, must soon deprive us of even the shadow of liberty, and of everything that is dear and valuable to English-men; And, being of the opinion, that it

so were based on honest conviction. That there was less sympathy for the American cause among the British merchants in 1769 than there had been in 1765 is unmistakable, and there is nothing to account for it except the advance in the American claims. Thomas Hutchinson, who represented conservative opinion, wrote to Israel Williams of Hatfield, May 9, 1769: "If we could be prudent, I think I may say only silent, we might save the country and retain the rights we contend for or which is the same thing might rest assured that parliament would not exercise the right of taxing which they claim, and we may be assured will not give up, but if we will go on denying the right and asserting our independence the nation will by force compell us to acknowledge it. I wish this force may be kept off as long as you and I live" (Williams Papers).

[1] I have not been able to find a copy of the Philadelphia resolutions. That such were drawn up at the meetings mentioned above is clear from later allusions. For example, certain shipments were declared contrary "to the agreements entered into by the merchants and traders of this city on February 6 and March 10" (Pennsylvania Chronicle, July 24, 1769). On August 2, the merchants of Philadelphia met at the Coffee House and resolved "that the committee shall not be at liberty to receive and store any goods consigned after the agreement of the merchants here not to import was known in Great Britain nor such as were ordered after the 6th of February last" (ibid. August 7, 1769). On June 5, 1770, a meeting was held in Philadelphia at which it was voted to adhere to the agreement entered into March 10, 1769, "almost unanimously" (Pennsylvania Gazette, June 14, 1770). Drinker speaks definitely of the "agreement formed on the 10 of March" (Pennsylvania Magazine, xiv. 42). Stephen Collins gives the date of the first agreement as "2mo 1 1769." This may be an error for February 6, or it may be that the first agreement was drafted on the 1st and ratified on the 6th.

[2] South Carolina Gazette, October 12, 1769.

is not only lawful, but our indispensible duty, to use our utmost influence to avert the calamity, misery and slavery, impending over us, and all our bretheren in North-America; and apprehending that the agreements of the merchants, and traders of these colonies, not to import certain enumerated articles from any part of Great-Britain, until the said acts of parliament are repealed, are wise, just and salutary, and will have a great tendency to this end; DO hereby testify and declare our approbation of them to prefer the future welfare of their country to their present private emolument.

In order to contribute our mite to this public and patriotic work, and willing to co-operate, as far as in us lies, with those advocates and friends to liberty and their country, do hereby mutually promise, declare and agree, upon our word, honour, and the faith of Christians;

I. That from and after this date we will not import, or bring into any part of America, any goods, wares or merchandizes what soever, from Great-Britain, contrary to the spirit and intentions of the agreement of the merchants of the City of Philadelphia in the province of Pennsylvania

II. That we *never will* have any dealings, commerce or intercourse whatsoever, with *any man*, residing in any part of the British Dominions, who shall for lucre, or any other purpose, import, or bring, into any part of America, any article or thing contrary to the said agreement.

III. That any one of us, who shall *wilfully* break this compact, shall have his name published in the public news-papers as a betrayer of the civil and religious rights of Americans, and be for ever after deemed *infamous* and *an enemy* to this country.[1]

Thus step by step the northern colonies were closing their ports to British goods. Albany came in during the summer of 1769.[2]

---

[1] The following additional information is given by the newspaper:

We hear that a number of the principal freeholders of the said County, assembled at Christiana-Bridge, on Saturday last, in pursuance of notice given for that purpose, when the occasion of their meeting, the grievances complained of by North-Americans, and the most probable methods of obtaining redress, were opened, and fully explained, and the above compact was read, approved, and signed by all présent. It is said that it will soon be signed by every freeholder and freeman in the country, and that the other counties in that government will immediately follow the example.

Some resolutions were made, nemine contradicente, in favour of persons, not inhabitants of the county, who should be so weak as to import any goods there contrary to the agreement; particularly, that they should be stored, effectually secured, and taken care of, until the obnoxious acts of parliament were repealed, except the same should be prevented by the imprudence of the owners.

[2] Albany acted very much under the influence of New York, but the merchants

Salem, Marblehead, and Gloucester had already adopted the Boston terms, and New Haven, which had received an urgent letter from New York in April, now on July 10th entered the ranks.[1] Though Nantucket refused to bind herself formally by any engagement, her merchants were in spirit and practice sympathetic to the cause. The Connecticut assembly on October 9, 1769, passed resolutions expressing warm approval of the agreements,[2] and on the 18th the New Jersey assembly formally extended its thanks to New York and Philadelphia for "their disinterested and public spirited conduct." [3] Providence gave in her accession on October 10th,[4] Newport on October 30th,[5] Wethersfield on December 25th,[6] Middletown [7] on February 20, 1770, Watertown [8] in March, and Falmouth (Portland) on June 26th of that year.[9] Many inland towns, such as Lancaster, Pennsylvania, which received their goods from the seaboard importers, agreed not to deal with those who broke the compact.[10] In the country districts where non-importation was a matter of less serious consequence than it was in the seaports, the plan was seized upon with avidity, and the town meetings passed resolutions, often

there wished to include among the exempted commodities such Indian goods as blankets, strouds, penistones, gimps, linens, vermilions, and brass kettles. The New York merchants would not agree to this and compelled them to adopt the New York plan. There is some uncertainty as to the date, but it was before July, 1769. Some of the Albany merchants were restless under this agreement, as the increasing scarcity of Indian goods not only interfered with trade, but also rendered less cordial the relations with the Indians, who suspected a conspiracy against themselves and could not understand why the traffic in furs stopped and presents were no longer given. See p. 240, below. Albany undoubtedly broke the agreement early, by importing what she wanted through Quebec and Montreal.

[1] Pennsylvania Chronicle, July 31, 1769; Boston Gazette, August 6, 1770. The New Haven agreement was signed by all at the meeting and was distributed to all in the town and the adjoining neighborhood.

[2] Connecticut Colonial Records, xiii. 236 note.

[3] New Jersey Archives, xxvi. 546.

[4] Providence Gazette, October 14, 21, 1769. Staples gives the date October 24. The meeting of the 10th was probably that of the merchants.

[5] Newport Mercury, November 6, 1769; Newport Historical Magazine, iii. 253-257.

[6] Wethersfield Town Records, under date, printed in Stiles, Ancient Wethersfield, i. 419-420.

[7] Middletown Town Records, under date.

[8] Boston Record Commissioners' Reports, xviii. 8.

[9] Boston Gazette, June 9, 1770. Text in full.

[10] Massachusetts Gazette and Boston News Letter, July 5, 1770.

extravagant and denunciatory, against the importation of English and Scottish goods.[1] Portsmouth alone of all the seaports of the North remained open to British trade. Though many attempts were made to bring the merchants there into line, beginning with the town meeting of July 8, 1768, and the first call of a merchants' meeting on September 12th, no decision was reached and Portsmouth remained permanently outside the movement.[2]

The South, though acting more slowly, was already keenly alive to the significance of what was taking place. Conditions there were in some ways essentially different from those in the North, for the grievances of the tobacco and rice colonies were bound to vary from those of the bread and provision colonies. The South suffered much less than the Middle Colonies and New England from the trade restrictions and could present no such series of grievances as had been drawn up by the Boston merchants. But the South did suffer from the scarcity of money, and was as deeply impressed as were the colonists anywhere with the so-called illegal and oppressive features of British policy. The southerners were equally ready to encourage frugality, promote manufactures, oppose importation, denounce unconstitutionality, uphold liberty and self-government, and persecute those who differed from them as enemies of the country, as were those of the North, but they omitted many features of the agreements that the North had included, included at least one, regarding negroes, that the North had omitted, and in the case of the tobacco colonies defined non-importation in terms that were much less re-

[1] New York Gazette or Weekly Post Boy, July 20, 1769; Boston Gazette, July 31, 1769. One of the most remarkable series of resolutions is that of Abington, Mass. Section 9 reads: "Voted as the opinion of this town that the agreement of the merchants and traders of the Town of Boston relative to non-importation has a natural and righteous tendency to frustrate the scheme of the enemies of the constitution, and to render ineffectual the said unconstitutional and unrighteous acts, and is a superlative instance of self-denial and public virtue, which we hope will be handed down to posterity, even to the latest generation, to their immortal honour" (Essex Gazette, April 3, 1770). These resolves gave the New York brethren "infinite pleasure." "How many ages hence," they said, "in unborn states and with accents yet unknown, shall these manly and noble resolves be recited" (ibid. May 5, 1770).

[2] The Portsmouth merchants were summoned to meet at the house of John Stavers, September 12, 1768, but want of accord led to the postponement of the meeting to the 16th, then to the 23d, and then indefinitely (New Hampshire Gazette, September 9, 1768). See pp. 233 note 1, 239, below.

strictive. The resolutions of Maryland, Virginia, and North Carolina were essentially the same in principle. Instead of promising to import no British goods, with a few exemptions, they allowed the "associators" to import all British goods except such as were carefully specified and such as were taxed by parliament, and they limited the operation of the agreement to the time when the repeal of the acts should take place. Thus the three "associations" were less rigid in their terms than were the agreements of the North, and left the merchants free to import many goods that the northerners bound themselves to exclude.

The first non-importation agreement entered into south of Pennsylvania and Delaware was that of Virginia. Early in April, 1769, Dr. Ross of Bladensburg forwarded to Washington at Mount Vernon the resolves of the Philadelphia merchants, and he in turn sent them to his neighbor, George Mason at Gunston Hall, recommending them for consideration. The latter agreeing with Ross and Washington that something ought to be done, drafted a body of resolutions, suitable for the colony. These resolutions were adopted on May 18, 1769, by the members of the House of Burgesses, which had just been dissolved by the governor, Lord Botetourt, for protesting against parliamentary taxation, and by certain merchants and traders who happened to be in Williamsburg at the time, eighty-eight altogether, meeting in the house of Anthony Hay. After a long preamble and an opening frugality clause, the resolutions proceed as follows:

Secondly, That they will not at any time hereafter, directly or indirectly, import or cause to be imported any manner of goods, merchandise, or manufactures, which are or shall hereafter be taxed by act of parliament for the purpose of raising a revenue in America (except paper not exceeding eight shillings sterling per ream and except such articles only as orders have been already sent for) nor purchase any such after the first day of September next, of any persons whatsoever. . . .

Thirdly, That the subscribers will not hereafter, directly or indirectly, import or cause to be imported, from Great Britain or any part of Europe . . . any of the goods hereinafter enumerated, viz, spirits, wine, cider, perry, beer, ale, malt, barley, pease, beef, pork, fish, butter, cheese, tallow, candles, oil, fruit, sugar, pickles, confectionary, pewter, hoes, axes, watches, clocks, tables, chairs, looking glasses, carriages, joiners and cabinet work of all sorts, upholstery of all sorts, trinkets and jewellery, plate and gold, and silversmiths' work of all sorts, ribband and millinery of all sorts, lace of all sorts, India goods of all sorts (except spices), silks of all sorts (except sewing silk), cambric, lawn, muslin, gauze (except bolting cloths), calico or cotton stuffs of more than two shillings per yard, linen of more than two shillings per yard, woolens, worsted stuffs of all sorts of more than one shilling and sixpence per yard, broad cloths of all kinds at more than eight shillings per yard, narrow cloths of all kinds at more than three shillings per yard, hats, stockings (plaid and Irish hose excepted), shoes and boots, saddles, and all manufactures of leather and skins of all kinds, until the late acts of parliament imposing on tea, paper, glass, etc, for the purpose of raising a revenue in America are repealed. . . .

Fourthly, That in all orders which any of the subscribers may hereafter send to Great Britain, they shall and will expressly direct their correspondents not to ship them any of the before enumerated goods until the before mentioned acts of parliament are repealed; and if any goods are shipped to them, contrary to the tenour of this agreement, they will refuse to take the same, or make themselves chargeable therewith.

Fifthly, That they will not import any slaves, or purchase any imported, after the first day of November next, until the said acts are repealed.

Sixthly, That they will not import wines of any kind whatever. . . .

Seventhly, For the better preservation of the breed of sheep, that they will not kill or suffer to be killed, any lambs that shall be weaned before the first day of May, in any year. . . .

Eighthly and lastly, That these resolves shall be binding on all and each of the subscribers. . . .[1]

Maryland came in about a month later. On the day after the meeting at Williamsburg, the merchants of Ann Arundel county issued a call for a convention to be held at Annapolis on May 23d. There the "associators" bound themselves not to send any orders to Great Britain until June 30th and not to import any goods whatever "contrary to the spirit and design of the association." Similar associations were organized in the other counties. Finally on June 22, 1769, representatives from all the counties came together at Annapolis and entered into a general agreement similar to that of Virginia. It was more elaborate, emphasized more conspicuously

[1] Printed in the Boston Chronicle, June 8, 1769, and in Burk, History of Virginia, iii. 345–349.

the constitutional claim, had a much more detailed list of commodities not to be imported, with more exemptions, and a more rigorous local boycotting clause. It also left out the fifth clause of the Virginia resolutions and added another binding the "tradesmen and manufactures" not to raise prices, but to sell everything at the accustomed rates. The agreement was signed by forty-three persons.[1]

South Carolina was reported to be ready to enter into a non-importation agreement as early as March, 1769, and the merchants and planters of Charles Town were looking seriously into the question of superfluities, the drain of money, and the amount spent for slaves, but it was not until June 27th that a body of the inhabitants, including twenty-five members of the general assembly, adopted a set of non-importation resolutions, and about ten days later that the merchants adopted another version. After considerable manœuvring, the two plans were consolidated and agreed upon at a general meeting on July 22d. This consolidated plan had been framed the week before by a joint committee and was designed to comprise all the essential parts of the two forms already adopted and circulated for subscribers. The new resolutions were signed by one hundred and forty-two planters, merchants, and mechanics, and a committee of about forty was selected to give force to the association.[2] The preamble and resolutions are as follows:

We, His Majesty's dutiful and loving Subjects, the Inhabitants of South-Carolina, being sensibly affected with the great Prejudice done to Great Britain, and the abject and wretched condition to which the British Colonies are reduced by several Acts of Parliament lately passed; by *some of which* the Monies that the Colonists usually and chearfully

---

[1] "The Proceedings of the Committee appointed to examine into the Importation of Goods by the Brigandine Good Intent Capt. Errington, from London in February, 1770," Annapolis, 1770. Reprinted in the Maryland Magazine, iii. nos. 2, 3, 4. See also the Eden-Hillsborough correspondence (ibid. ii. 228–229, 234, 239, 244). The resolutions are printed in this pamphlet (Maryland Magazine, iii. 144–147); Maryland Gazette, June 29, 1769; Boston Chronicle, July 10, 1769; and Scharf, History of Maryland, i. 111–114.

[2] South Carolina Gazette, June 29, July 6, 27, 1769. The early history of the South Carolina draft is confusing. John Gordon wrote that the resolutions of July 22 were the seventh form of agreement and the fifth to be subscribed, and though he was one of the first to coöperate, he was tired of being bandied about from resolution to resolution (South Carolina Gazette, September 14, 1769).

spent in the Purchase of all Sorts of Goods imported from Great Britain, are now, to their great Grievance, wrung from them, without their Consent, or even their being representated, and applied by the Ministry, in Prejudice of, and without Regard to, the real Interest of Great-Britain, or the Manufactures thereof, almost totally, to the Support of new-created Commissioners of Customs, Placemen, parasitical and novel ministerial Officers; and *by others of which Acts*, we are not only deprived of those invaluable Rights, Trial by our Peers and the Common Law, but are also made subject to the arbitrary and oppressive Proceedings of the Civil Law, justly abhorred and rejected by our Ancestors, the Free-Men of England; and finding, that the most dutiful and loyal Petitions from the Colonies Alone, for Redress of those Grievances, have been rejected with Contempt, so that no Relief can be expected from that Method of Proceedings; and, being fully convinced of the absolute Necessity, of stimulating our Fellow-Subjects and Sufferers in Great-Britain to aid us, in this our Distress, and of joining the Rest of the Colonies, in some other loyal and vigorous Methods, that may most probably procure such Relief, which we believe may be most effectually promoted by strict Oeconomy, and by encouraging the Manufactures of America in general, and of this Province in particular: We therefore, whose names are underwritten, do solemnly promise, and agree to and with each other, That, until the Colonies be restored to their former Freedom, by the Repeal of the said Acts, we will most strictly abide by the following

RESOLUTIONS

I. That we will encourage and promote the Use of North-American Manufactures in general, and those of this Province in particular. And any of us, who are Venders thereof, do engage to sell and dispose of them, at the same Rates as heretofore.

II. That we will upon no Pretence whatsoever, either upon our own Account or on Commission, import into this Province any of the Manufactures of Great-Britain, or any other European or East-India Goods, either from Great Britain, Holland, or any other Place, other than such as may have been Shipped in Consequence of former Orders; excepting only Negro Cloth, commonly called white and coloured Plains, not exceeding one Shilling and Six Pence Sterling per Yard, Canvas, Bolting Cloths, Drugs and Family Medicines, Plantation and Workmens Tools, Nails, Fire Arms, Bar Steel, Gun Powder, Shot, Lead, Flints, Wire Cards and Card wire, Mill and Grind Stones, Fish hooks, printed Books and Pamphlets, Salt, Coals, and Salt-Petre. And exclusive of these articles, we do solemnly promise and declare, that we will immediately countermand all Orders to our Correspondents in Great-Britain, for shipping any Such Goods, Wares and Merchandize: And we will sell and dispose of the Goods we have on Hand, or that may arrive in Consequence of former Orders at the same rates as heretofore.

III. That we will use the utmost Oeconomy, in our Persons, Houses and Furniture; particularly, that we will give no mourning, or Gloves, or Scarves at Funerals,

IV. That, from and after the 1st. Day of January, 1770, we will not import, buy, or sell, any Negroes that shall be brought into this Province from Africa; nor, after the 1st. Day of October next, any Negroes that shall be imported from the West-Indies, or any other Place excepting from Africa as aforesaid: And that, if any Goods or Negroes shall be sent to us, contrary to our Agreement in this Subscription such Goods shall be re-shipped or stored, and such Negroes re-shipped from this Province, and not by any Means offered for Sale therein.

V. That we will not purchase from, or sell for, any Masters of Vessels, transient Persons, or Non-Subscribers, any Kind of European or East-India Goods whatever, excepting Coals and Salt, after the 1st Day of November next:

VI. That as Wines are subject to a heavy Duty, we agree, not to import any on our Account or Commission, or purchase from any Master of Vessel, transient Person, or Non-Subscriber, after the 1st. Day of January next.

VII. Lastly, That we will not purchase any Negroes imported, or any Goods or Merchandize whatever, from any Resident in this Province, that refuses or neglects to sign this Agreement, within one Month from the Date hereof; excepting it shall appear he has been unavoidably prevented from doing the same. And every Subscriber who shall not, strictly and literally adhere to this Agreement, according to the true Intent and Meaning hereof, ought to be treated with the utmost Contempt.

Georgia and North Carolina entered the list last of all in the order named, and while the agreement of the latter followed in the main those of Virginia and Maryland, the agreement of the former was in principle similar to those of South Carolina and the northern cities. Such alignment was the natural outcome of the economic relations of the colonies to each other, for North Carolina, except in the Cape Fear section, had generally identified herself with the tobacco colonies to the northward, while South Carolina and Georgia had many interlocking interests. The news of the non-importation movement reached Savannah as early as October, 1767,[1] but it was not until September 12, 1769, that a body of merchants, planters, and tradesmen, possibly aroused by protests from Charles Town, met at the house of Mr. Peat and chose a committee to draft resolutions. This committee reported on the 19th a form of agreement similar to the one later ratified, in which they promised not to import any English, European, or East Indian goods, except a certain number carefully enumerated, including goods for the Indian trade.[2] On the 16th the merchants had met separately at the house of Alexander Creighton, and had drawn up a statement of grievances, followed by a resolve that any person importing articles subject to parliamentary taxation should be deemed an enemy to his country.[3] Shortly afterwards, at a public meeting held in Savannah, with Jonathan Bryan in the chair, a final agreement was entered into, which was modelled after that of South Carolina, but was differently worded in the preamble

---

[1] Georgia Gazette, October 26, 1769.

[2] Georgia Gazette, September 13, 20, 1769.

[3] "It was agreed, That the late acts so fully and unanimously remonstrated against by the Northern Colonies were in themselves unconstitutional and the mode of taxation was entirely inconsistent with the abilities of the people.

"At a time when we believe that healing measures and a redress of grievances will be effectually pursued at the next meeting of Parliament, we think it unnecessary to enumerate the whole, further than that, in general, and as far as we know, we approve of and agree in sentiment with the other provinces.

"It was agreed respecting this province in particular that the mode of payment of such duties is a great additional grievance. The sterling current money of this province, which was by Act of Assembly assented to by his Majesty and declared equal in value to the sterling money of Great Britain and a lawful tender in all payments, being refused in payment of such duties, tends greatly to depreciate its value; a circumstance greatly affecting every person anywise interested in this province; after having WISELY excluded us [from] the Spanish trade, the only channel through which specie could possibly be procured, and then, by subsequent acts imposing duties on us payable in *gold and silver*, shews that they are entirely ignorant of our internal police, and know little of what is beneficial to the colonies, and thereby prevents our having it even in our power to give a regular and constitutional aid to the mother country, if such was demanded.

"WE THEREFORE RESOLVE, That any person or persons whatever, importing any of the articles subject to such duties, after having it in their power to prevent it, ought not only to be treated with the utmost contempt, but deemed enemies to their country, it being a circumstance that would need only to be mentioned to any person, inspired with the least sense of liberty that it may be detested and abhorred" (Georgia Gazette, September 20, 1769; Tobler, South Carolina and Georgia Almanack, for 1770).

and in general much more concisely expressed.[1] The Georgia agreement, like that of South Carolina, represented the combined action of the merchants, planters, and people at large.

In North Carolina the situation was very much like that of Virginia. The assembly was dissolved by Governor Tryon on November 6, 1769. Immediately sixty-four of the seventy-seven members met in the court-house at New Bern, organized themselves as a convention, and appointed a committee to draw up a set of resolutions. The committee's report was presented on the 7th and formally adopted. The agreement followed that of Virginia, laying less stress on the constitutional claim than did that of Maryland, binding the subscribers not to import slaves, leaving the door open for the importation of Indian goods, as did all the southern colonies, and copying in all but a few particulars the very language of its exemplar.[2] With the accession of North Carolina to the ranks of the non-importers, the chain of the colonies was complete. By November, 1769, every one of the original thirteen colonies except New Hampshire, and all of the more important cities except Portsmouth, had either joined the movement or expressed its sympathy with it. Quebec, Montreal, Nova Scotia, and the Floridas did not raise the issue at all.

VI

When the agreement had once been signed, the procedure followed was everywhere pretty much the same. The first object was to obtain subscribers, for which purpose blanks were distributed widely and considerable pressure of a legitimate character was brought to bear on those who hesitated or refused. While many signed the papers with enthusiasm, others yielded from a sense of duty or for fear of the consequences. Merchants, tradesmen, retailers, wharfingers, and the like, who held out against all persuasion, were deemed enemies to their country, and were avoided

---

[1] Revolutionary Records of Georgia, i. 8–11. The list of exemptions was somewhat different, including in addition osnaburgs, certain varieties of flannels, linen, hose, cottons, checks, felt hats, shoes, hardware of all sorts (probably the same as "plantation and workman's tools, nails, and fishhooks" which are in the South Carolina list and omitted from that of Georgia), paper, and Indian goods. The list omits also salt and bar-steel.

[2] South Carolina Gazette, December 8, 1769; Connor, North Carolina Booklet, viii. 21–26; Connor, Cornelius Harnett, pp. 53–57.

socially, excommunicated politically, and boycotted in business. In the same class with non-subscribers were "informers," "violators" of the agreements, and "revolters" who had broken through, as in New York. If they refused to yield or became aggressive in their resistance, they were liable to coercion and maltreatment, their shops and wharves to damage, and themselves to indignity and suffering. Some were tarred and feathered, carted through the streets, or driven out of town, as in Boston, Salem, and New Haven; some were hung in effigy, as in Boston, New York, and Charles Town; some were stood under the gallows, and others were ducked in the nearest pond.[1] Those who dealt with non-subscribers or "violators" were always under suspicion and sometimes had to clear themselves by advertisement, lest their business be ruined.[2] The number of those treated in this manner is not large, many who were threatened made voluntary submission, others acquitted themselves before the committees of charges presented by over-zealous persons without sufficient knowledge, while in at least one case where the mob burned goods in storage, the indignant sufferer brought suit against the committee and was awarded damages.[3]

In the South, where the associations were the work of the planters

---

[1] For the case of Adonijah Thomas of West Haven, see the New London Gazette, September 20, 1769; for cases in Boston, Rowe, Diary, October 28, 1769, May 18, 1770, March 9, 1775. Tar and feathers were kept on hand in New Jersey (New Jersey Archives, xxvii. 217; see also the Holyoke Diaries, p. 69). Two New York "revolters," who went to New Brunswick, N. J., were stopped and "genteely ducked" at Woodbridge (New York Journal, August 9, 1770; New Jersey Archives, xxvii. 218, 220).

[2] "Resolved, That every subscriber who shall presume directly or indirectly to *purchase from* or *sell for* any violator of the general resolutions, shall be looked upon in the same odious light as a violator himself, shunned as a pestilence and held in the utmost abhorrence and contempt" (South Carolina Gazette, June 28, 1770). For illustration, see Letters of James Murray, Loyalist, p. 179.

The following is a good specimen of the language used in denouncing violators: "Gibetted (in Fame) to rot and stink under the noses of their countrymen, as a mark of public infamy and warning to those who shall endeavour to counteract the designs of society in favour of Liberty. If oppression, according to Solomon, maketh a wise man mad, what a pity 'tis that it cannot teach fools wisdom."

[3] The case of David Hill of Massachusetts, whose barrels of goods were seized by a mob in New York and burnt. This action called out a protest and denunciation from the committee of inspection (New York Gazette or Weekly Post Boy, July 9, 1770). Hill brought suit against the committee of merchants, Isaac Low and others, and was awarded £280 damages in March, 1772.

and radicals as well as of the merchants, there were large numbers who refused to conform. Probably a majority of the merchants of Norfolk was in opposition to the Virginia association, and in Wilmington and Charles Town, where the movement was dominated by the Sons of Liberty from the beginning, the merchants though acquiescing showed no great enthusiasm.[1] There was less hounding of non-subscribers in the South than in the North, but the same efforts were made in both sections to break down opposition.

In order to prevent the importation of British and other goods contrary to the agreements, subscribers in the North and associators in the South appointed committees of inspection, whose business it was to watch for violations, to examine manifests and cargoes, and to bring doubtful cases before the general body for consideration and settlement. In nearly every city and colony, goods were seized and stored under the direction of such committees, generally in private warehouses, the keys of which were given up, or else such goods were sent back to England or to the colony from whence they came. It was the early practice, particularly in the North, to store the goods, but later, in Maryland, Virginia, and South Carolina, and to a considerable extent in Boston and Philadelphia, they were returned. In some cases ships were not allowed to come to dock, if they were suspected of having forbidden goods on board, and it was deemed important and necessary that the owners of wharves and their wharfingers should be favorable to the cause. In some cases vessels went on from port to port vainly seeking an entry. The Sharpe went to New York, then to Philadelphia, then to Norfolk, but was sent away from each place; the Tristram, sent away from Providence, went to Wethersfield, where the importer was compelled to store the goods.[2] In several cases, the importers broke into the warehouses and carried off their own goods,[3] and in one instance at

---

[1] This is the impression one gets from a study of the Laurens Papers and from the report of the Wilmington meeting of the Sons of Liberty, July 5, 1770, when many of the merchants refused to sign the agreement (Cape Fear Mercury, July 11, 1770). A Charles Town merchant writing to his correspondent in England said that those who got up the agreement there were men without credit in England.

[2] Stiles, Wethersfield, i. 418–419.

[3] The cases of Gov. Hutchinson's sons in Boston (Massachusetts Papers, pp. 131–132) and Peter Frye and others in Salem (Essex Gazette, October 2, 1770).

least a mob defied the committee, broke open the warehouse, and burnt the goods.[1] There was much running of forbidden commodities by night, and the charge was freely made that the warehouses had two doors, one in front and one behind, and where one case of the kind is recorded, there must have been many of which the committees had no knowledge.[2]

We are now ready to return to the situation in Boston. On August 1, 1768, the agreement had been signed, committing the merchants to the policy of non-importation, which marked the first line of cleavage in the old Society, between subscribers and non-subscribers. The rift thus made widened when in November rumors got abroad that the merchants in Salem, Marblehead, and Cape Ann were breaking their agreements, and the Standing Committee on January 19, 1769, wrote to Peter Frye, chairman of the merchants' committee in Salem, asking for information.[3] Though the rumor was denied,

---

[1] Above, p. 222 note 3.

[2] A writer to the New York Gazette or Weekly Post Boy, August 27, 1770, said that in Newport and Boston every store had two doors, which made it easy to keep the agreement. He said also that the stores were often open and that many thousands of dollars were taken from Connecticut and adjacent counties in the night time. Newport denied vehemently that there were "back doors to the public stores."

Illustrations could be given of goods stored or returned in every colony. The most active towns were Charles Town, Annapolis, Philadelphia, New York, and Boston. In Charles Town there was a committee of inspection that covered the coast from Georgetown (Winyah) to Beaufort, and in Maryland and Virginia there were committees of inspection for each county. Some of the best known cases are: Boston, Capt. Scott, Capt. Bryant (the Wolf); Providence, Capt. Shand (the Tristram); New York, Capt. Speir (the Sharpe), Capt. Munds (the Brittania); Middletown, Conn., Capt. Butler; Philadelphia, Capt. Strickland (the Speedwell); Baltimore, Capt. Johnson (the Lord Cambden); Annapolis, Capt. Bryson (the Betsey), Capt. Carter (the Flora), Capt. Errington (the Good Intent). From Georgetown various colonial vessels were sent back, and from Charles Town, vessels from Boston, New York, and Jamaica, and those importing goods for Saxby, Gillon, Benjamin and Ann Matthews, Stukes, and Tidyman. There is much in the Collins Papers about the ship Commerce from Hull to New York and Philadelphia. Many cases are recorded in which the names are not given, as when Maryland compelled an owner to reship twenty pipes of wine, and Philadelphia prevented a cargo from being landed, which was to have been got ashore in small parcels and in different parts. Ample evidence exists for a study of these and other cases, but they cannot be considered further here.

[3] To Peter Frye and other Gentlemen of the Committee of Merchants, Salem, Jan. 19, 1769: "Being informed by letters from Salem that some persons there who signed the agreement for the non-importation of goods have, contrary to

the committee continued its inquiries, and on April 21st was able to report to the Body that only nine out of two hundred and eleven had imported. The Body then appointed a special inspection committee of seven to examine the manifests of the cargoes and to make further report. This the committee did at an adjourned meeting on the 27th, stating that but seven subscribers had imported, with eight non-subscribers and five sea captains,[1] and that the number, though larger than could be wished, was inconsiderable and the quantity and value of the goods were very small. It warned the public that "the purchasing of any kind of English goods brought from other colonies since January, 1769," was contrary to the agreement. In consequence of this warning a number of the subscribers turned over for storage goods that had evidently been imported under a misunderstanding.[2]

But the non-subscribers refused to yield, and a determined campaign was begun against them. In May, with the design of casting public odium upon them, a printed paper was handed about, containing the names of eleven merchants who refused to conform, and recommending that all citizens should avoid them. Alarmed at reports of the influence which Hillsborough's letter of May 13th, promising the repeal of the acts in part, was having on the moderates in the town, the Standing Committee met at the Coffee House on June 24th and prepared a new agreement according to which the

---

said agreement, sent their Spring orders and others are preparing to do the same, alledging that Marblehead and Cape Ann havent come into the agreement, and that in case other towns did not and any in Salem should not conform to it others were not held," the committee said that this conduct had caused great uneasiness, and they wished to inform Salem that Marblehead and Cape Ann had come in, New York was holding fast, Boston was more determined than ever, and their best friends in England approved (Massachusetts Historical Society, O2517, no. 63).

[1] The sea captains and masters made considerable trouble. In South Carolina it was found that "the Resolutions had been in some measure defeated by masters of vessels and other transient persons being at liberty to dispose of goods they imported if they could find purchasers, several persons having availed themselves of this opening and clandestinely disposed of and purchased, and others refused to store or reship goods thus imported." On this account the Body of Merchants entered into a new agreement designed to put a stop to this evil. This agreement was repeated in March, 1770 (South Carolina Gazette, February 1, March 8, 1770).

[2] Massachusetts Historical Society, O2517, nos. 40, 43, 63.

arrangement of August 1st was to remain in force unless all the revenue acts, those of 1764 and 1766 as well as the Townshend Act, should be repealed. Two days later, the Body met and, renewing the agreement of August 1st, voted unanimously that the removal of the duties on glass, paper, and painters' colors was not enough, but that all the acts must be repealed. The Body appointed three committees, one to increase subscriptions, one to inspect cargoes, and one to prepare a state of trade grievances.[1] This action of the merchants was merely a renewal of the old agreement, but it probably had the effect of creating further dissensions among themselves. Evidently these differences found expression, particularly on the part of non-subscribers, for on August 11th the Body met and voted that the scheme was likely to be efficacious only if adhered to. They denounced as "enemies to trade, their neighbors, and their country" all who continued to import, and declared that if such persons would not submit, their names would be published in the newspapers.

In consequence of this threat, six of the fourteen non-subscribing firms yielded, but eight refused, and their names were printed in four Boston papers and the Essex Gazette. They were Richard Clark & Son, John Bernard, Nathaniel Rogers, Theophilus Lillie, James McMasters & Co., John Mein, Thomas Hutchinson, Jr., and Elisha Hutchinson.[2] Of the eight thus publicly denounced, all but three came in later, leaving John Bernard, James McMasters & Co., and John Mein defiant and refusing even to attend the merchants' meeting. Two more names were added at a meeting of the merchants in November, Henry Barnes of Marlborough,[3] and Ame and Elizabeth Cuming of Boston, and in December four merchants of Marblehead, who refused to enter the agreement there and continued to import and offer for sale, were published in the Boston papers.[4]

---

[1] Rowe, Diary, July 24, 1769; Boston Chronicle, July 27, 1769; Boston Gazette, July 31, 1769.

[2] Boston Gazette, August 14, 1769. The Boston town meeting aided the merchants by entering these names on the records of its session of October 4 (Boston Record Commissioners' Reports, xvi. 298).

[3] For the sufferings of Henry Barnes, see the letter from Mrs. Barnes, June, 1770, printed in Letters of James Murray, Loyalist, pp. 175–177.

[4] Boston Gazette, November 20, December 25, 1769. Colburn Barrell, who

This publishing of names in the public press gave rise to perhaps the most interesting and instructive incident of the whole non-importation movement, when one man, employing the press as his weapon and fortifying himself with facts and figures, defied the entire body of subscribers in Boston. John Mein, a Scotsman, had come to New England in October, 1764, and in 1765 opened a book store and circulating library in King Street, just above the British Coffee House on the north side.[1] In 1767, he started the Boston Chronicle, one of the best planned and best written of the Boston newspapers, and a year later was chosen stationer to the American Board of Customs Commissioners.[2] He had refused to join in the

---

had subscribed, said afterwards that he was bullied into the agreement "by the threatening and cajoling conduct of some of their committee men." He did not wish to have trouble with the merchants, desiring to live quietly and at peace with his fellow townsmen. He was willing to reship, if the merchants would meet all charges for insurance and freight and would recompense him for damage incurred in returning the goods (compare the same proposition made by James Dick in the Good Intent case, Maryland Magazine, iii. 356). The committee replied, but Barrell said that the reply was insufficient and he proceeded to make remarks at some length, calling his submission unlawful and the meeting that asked for it unlawful. In consequence, he considered himself freed from his engagement. At a meeting of the merchants, held on December 7, this letter was commented upon severely. Barrell replied that there were many non-subscribing merchants in Boston and those who yielded to threats were cowards. Barrell showed a good deal of courage. He had been a merchant of Newmarket, N. H., and a member of the Sandemanian church of Portsmouth (Sandeman-Barrell Papers), and was a brother of William, Joseph, and Walter Barrell. He had a shop just north of the Mill-bridge (Boston Chronicle, October 9, December 7, 1769).

The New Yorkers about this time advertised one Simeon Cooley, a jeweller, who having joined the merchants later defied them, and broke the agreement. The subscribers called on the people to boycott him as "the most insolent, impertinent, and daring of any former aggressor." Cooley eventually submitted (New York Gazette and Weekly Mercury, July 24, 1769). Similarly Thomas Richardson, jeweller, was compelled to retract (New York Journal, September 21, 1769). Jewellers seem to have been particularly obstinate. Philip Tidyman of Charles Town was a jeweller (South Carolina Gazette, November 1, 1770).

[1] See Mr. Bolton's article in Publications of this Society, xi. 196–200, and notes on p. 200, also p. 6 note 4. The facts of Mein's career are well known and need not be rehearsed here, but extracts will be given from his memorial to the Treasury, which has never been used.

[2] Mein said that before 1769 he "carried on in his various occupations of bookseller, stationer, and printer, the most extensive trade of any person on the American Continent" and "possessed the confidence of the Principal People." His paper had a subscription list of fourteen hundred and his bookstore netted

non-importation movement at the time of the Stamp Act, and again refused in 1768, though urgently requested to do so.[1] In consequence of this refusal, he was persecuted by the merchants, who exerted all their influence to ruin him. "They applied to his customers to desert him, they ʃent to the selectmen of every town in the province to promote subscriptions not to deal with him, and they held him up in anonymous handbills and in anonymous advertisements in the newspapers as an enemy to America." In retaliation he "adopted the plan of exposing them, to accomplish which he printed in his newspaper the manifests of all the cargoes of the vessels that had arrived in the port of Boston from Great Britain since the commencement of the non-importation agreement," and these, to the number of 4000 sheets of the principal importations, he circulated over all America, from Florida to Nova Scotia. In addition he printed 500 copies of the whole in a quarto pamphlet, one half of which he succeeded in distributing.[2] The result was that

---

him £40, £60, and £80 a week, while his stock in trade amounted to six or seven thousand pounds sterling (Public Record Office, Treasury 1: 478, f. 478).

[1] "The speaker of the House of Representatives, and many others, the Heads of the Faction, harrassed him daily for months, first with entreaties, urging as strong motive the great encouragement he had received among them, and afterwards employed threats, in order to induce him to accede to their combination. He was even told that the Crisis was now arrived, in which Neutrality was criminal, but he remained uniform in his refusal, a Sense of Duty being more prevalent with him than either the continuance or the increased favour of the public, which he was led to expect, or their highest displeasure, with which he was threatened" (ibid.).

[2] Mein was aroused by the report of the committee stating that but few importations had taken place, and by the decision of the Body to print the names of delinquents. In his own paper (August 17, 1769) he left blank the space where the names should have been. He began to print the manifests of importations, since January 1, 1769, on August 21 and continued them on the 24, 28, 31, September 4, 7, 11, 14, 18, etc., to October 19, with a running commentary. On December 11, 14, 18, he added the manifest of the ship John, owned by John Hancock, and manifests of other vessels owned by Boston merchants, and he continued publishing the manifests in January and February, 1770, issuing fifty-five in all. Furthermore he gave a list of forty non-signers, who made heavy importations during the year. As stated above, he issued these manifests in a pamphlet entitled "A State of the Importations from Great Britain into the Port of Boston from the Beginning of January, 1769, to August 17, 1769," with an Appendix of importations to January 1, 1770. The other side of the controversy can be followed in the Boston Gazette and in Massachusetts Historical Society, O2517, no. 65. On September 10, the merchants took his case into consideration and

a mass of incriminating evidence against the Boston merchants was spread broadcast throughout the country, raising, as Mein himself said, "distrust and dissenssion not only in the very heart of the Boston Faction, but between that Faction and the other combining colonies." Naturally Mein became obnoxious to the Bostonians, his subscribers fell off more than half, his bookselling business was ruined, the signs at his bookstore and printing office were besmeared with dirt, and he himself was treated as an informer and his effigy taken out with that of the Devil on November 5th or Pope

---

voted that he had endeavored to frustrate the good intentions of the signers of the agreement, by maliciously insinuating to the public that the agreement had not been generally complied with and that the committee's report was false and intended to deceive the public, and further that he had treated "the inspectors, the committee, and the whole body of merchants and traders in the most haughty, imperious, and insulting manner."

The influence of the facts Mein presented can hardly be overestimated, while in temper and good manners he distinctly had the best of his opponents. There is certainly nothing "scurrilous," "scandalous," "impudent," or "contemptible" in what Mein wrote in his paper, and the language used by the patriotic party and their laudation of themselves and their motives and characters arouse the suspicion that Mein's disclosures struck a tender spot. The weakness of the defence lies in its scurrility, its anonymity, its refusal to give names, and its concealment of the places where the goods were stored. It is curious how unwilling the upholders of non-importation were to sign their names to their articles. Conceding that anonymity was a fashion of the time, we must feel that the refusal to acknowledge authorship was a confession of weakness or worse. Hutchinson once said that such articles were the production of people "who if they would sign their names need do nothing more to blast the credit of everything they say" (Hutchinson to Williams, September 18, 1769, Williams Papers).

If Mein's facts are correct, then the merchants of Boston and Salem, and notably John Hancock, were doing a fairly prosperous freighting business in goods made contraband by the merchants. The explanations given by the latter are not convincing, and that they were not convincing to the merchants of New York and Philadelphia, the sequel was to prove. The latter frequently quoted Mein's sheets and pamphlet. In the face of the facts given, it is hardly a sufficient defence of Hancock to say that his "name will shine in the records of fame when infamous Jacobites and Tories will sink in oblivion," however true that statement may be as a prophecy (Boston Gazette, October 9, 1769). Mein was the first active opponent of the non-importation movement in America, and the information that he furnished did much to bring about its failure, for, as he says himself, "The Rupture between the Boston Faction and the combining colonies of N. York and Philadelphia will be evinced from their own advertisements; for the accusations brought by the latter against the former could be drawn from no other source than the publications of your Memorialist" (Public Record Office, Treasury 1: 478, f. 480).

71

Day.[1] Attacked by the mob, Mein in defence wounded a grenadier, and as warrants were issued against him he escaped to England. With his later career we are not concerned. Though deeply involved in financial difficulties, he returned to Boston, engaged again in business, and was twice posted for persisting in his refusal to join the movement. He left New England permanently some time after 1771.[2]

In the meantime information was received by the merchants that Philadelphia and New York were sending orders to England for goods to be shipped in case the acts should be repealed. As the

---

[1] The acrostic containing the line

> M ean is the man, M-n is his name

is printed in our Publications, xi. 198; and the "Description of the Pope, 1769," of which the acrostic forms a part, was printed in full in the Boston Chronicle, November 9, 1769, and also in a broadside. The following additional lines may be quoted:

> Here stands the Devil for a Show,
> With the I-p-rs in a row,
> All bound to Hell, and that we know.
> Go M-n lade deep with curses on thy head,
> To some dark Corner of the World repair,
> Where the bright Sun no pleasant Beams can shed,
> And spend thy Life in Horror and Despair.

At the head of the broadside is a rough woodcut, in which Mein's effigy, substituted for that of the Pope, appears standing under a gallows on a four-wheeled wagon, with the Devil behind, and before and after various smaller devils and tomcods. These are defined as "M-n, his Servant, &c. A Bunch of Tom-Cods." The following also is printed on the sheet:

"See the Informer, how he stands. If any one now takes his Part, An Enemy to all the Land, He'll go to Hell without a cart."

[2] Rowe, Diary, October 28, 1769; our Publications, xi. 198–200, where Mr. Bolton gives information regarding Mein's financial troubles, drawn from letters in private hands. His account should be studied in connection with Mein's remarks in his Memorial about justice in Massachusetts. There is a paper in the Dartmouth collection at Patshull House, containing information which Mein furnished John Pownall, under secretary of state for the colonies, but I have been unable to get a copy of it, because Patshull House is at present a military hospital. For the attack on Mein, see Hutchinson to Secretary Hillsborough, November 11, 1769, Colonial Office, 5:758, p. 445; Andrew Oliver to Sir Francis Bernard, same date, British Museum, Egerton, 2670, f. 28; and the London Chronicle, December 19, 1769. In the Letters of James Murray, Loyalist, pp. 168–174, are many references to Mein, whom Murray assisted. John Rowe notes the presence of "Mr. Murray of Cape Fear" at the Merchants' Club, May 27, 1765, and we may not doubt that he was in attendance at other times also.

Boston agreement was to expire at the end of the year, it was necessary to take action for the future, so on October 17th the merchants and traders met and considered what should be done. Feeling that the attitude of Philadelphia and New York did not sufficiently meet their own trade grievances, they voted that orders sent to Great Britain should be conditional, depending not on the repeal of the Townshend Act only but on the repeal of all the acts imposing duties for raising a revenue in America, and they hoped that the merchants elsewhere would come into a similar arrangement. When, however, it was found that the merchants of New York and Philadelphia had already ordered their goods to be shipped, in case the Townshend Act was repealed, and for this and other reasons refused to concur in the agreement of October 17th, proposing only to join in a plan for obtaining the repeal of the Acts of 1764 and 1766, the merchants of Boston, wishing to act in unison with the others, agreed to adopt the Philadelphia and New York plan.[1]

On November 7th, the Body voted that merchants might write to their correspondents instructing them to ship in case the Townshend Act was repealed.[2] As this vote was certain to antagonize those who had already laid plans for resuming importation after January 1, 1770, and would resent the extension of time which closed the door indefinitely, the meeting voted to publish the names of any shipping goods contrary to the agreement and to hold them up as persons "counteracting the salutary measures the merchants are pursuing to obtain a redress of grievances." Notwithstanding this vote, which was repeated on December 6th, the number of importers

---

[1] Massachusetts Papers, pp. 128–130; Boston Gazette, November 20, 1769; Letters of Dennys De Berdt, our Publications, xiii. 398–399. De Berdt wrote to Thomas McKean, February 15, 1770: "The condisinal orders (if these acts are repel'd) arose from the Quakers in Phil[a], who grew impatient of the restraints on tread, and came into this new agreement which they communicated to Boston & Boston has done the same."

[2] Boston Gazette, November 20, 1769; Massachusetts Historical Society, Broadsides, December 6, 1769. A considerable enlargement was made in the list of exempted articles. The additional articles in the new list are here italicized:

Coals, salt, fishhooks and lines, hemp and duck, bar-lead, shot, wool-cards and card wire, *clothier's shears, tin plates, drugs* and *medicines, dyestuffs, alum* and *copperas, gunpowder, grindstones, chalk, sheet-copper, German steel, schoolbooks,* as also "the article of *Bayze* for the supply of the fishing." The influence of the lists adopted by other colonies is clearly seen.

increased and became bolder. Rumors were prevalent that goods were illegally brought in and not stored as the agreement demanded. Complaints came from various quarters, and Newport and Providence, influenced by Mein's disclosures, charged Boston with violating the agreements.[1] The subscribers declared that all these accusations were but part of a "Tory scheme" to interrupt and destroy that "union and harmony" which alone could deliver America from her burdens.

Continued infractions [2] so alarmed the Trade that on January 16, 1770, a call was issued for a meeting of the Whole Body on the 17th, —

to receive the report of the committee of inspection relative to the most unaccountable and extraordinary conduct of three or four persons, some of whom have sold, others removed, and others threaten to sell their goods that have been stored, in direct violation of their solemn engagements to the contrary; and to consider and determine on some legal and spirited measures to prevent the non-importation agreement being rendered abortive by the machinations of those few persons, who by behaving in this perfidious manner will most audaciously counteract the whole Continent in the measures now pursuing for the preservation of their liberties.[3]

In consequence of this call, the merchants met at Faneuil Hall on January 17th, 18th, and 23d, and decided to break down all opposition by force, if necessary. On the 17th the Whole Body visited the house and store of William Jackson, on the 18th those of the Hutchinsons, Theophilus Lillie, John Taylor, Nathaniel Rogers, and Jackson again. On the 23d, the Hutchinsons having agreed to hand over their goods, they declared the remaining four, together with John Bernard, James and Patrick McMasters, Ame and Elizabeth Cuming, "obstinate and inveterate enemies to their country and subverters of the Rights and Liberties of this Continent," and

---

[1] Joseph Rotch & Son to Aaron Lopez, November 29, 1769: "We are now well assured that all the Agreements in the world will not prevent the Boston purchasers from exceeding the limits agreed on," and they want to know whether the "manufacturers of Newport intend altering their agreement or not" (Commerce of Rhode Island, i. 288. See also Boston Gazette, December 11, 1769).

[2] The Hutchinson and Sheafe affairs especially, for which see Massachusetts Papers, pp. 131–132, and Drake, History and Antiquities of Boston, p. 775.

[3] Massachusetts Historical Society, O2517; Broadsides, January 16, 1770.

they voted to boycott them and outlaw them from the country.[1] This action of the merchants, or, as we are justified in saying, of the radicals among them, seemed so akin to disorderly conduct and a disturbance of the peace that Lieutenant-Governor Hutchinson sent the sheriff to bid them disperse, but without effect.[2] The period was one of tremendous excitement in Boston,[3] the Boston Massacre

[1] Rowe, Diary under dates; Broadside, January 23, 1770. The broadside further says: "The friends of liberty and their country's cause are desired to paste this up over the Chimney Piece of every Public House and on every other proper place, in every Town in this and every other Colony, there to remain as a Monument of the Remembrance of the Detestable Names above mentioned." Another vote at the meeting was to this effect, "That the committee of inspection be directed to use their endeavours to discover the owner or owners of such goods upon their arrival, and being thus discovered, we will not sell or buy of, or have any dealings or social intercourse whatever with such persons for the space of two years, from the time of the arrival of such goods, and that the committee of inspection are desired to publish this vote, together with the names of the owners of such goods for the space of two years from the time of their arrival."

An example of such publication, relating to William Jackson, was given in our Publications, viii. 99 note.

Nathaniel Rogers in May, 1770, left Boston and went to New York, where the Sons of Liberty carried his effigy through the streets. Leaving New York, he went to Shelter Island, and there, word from New York having been received in advance, his effigy was placed on a pole, with the label "Nat. Rogers one of the infamous importers," and after being paraded through the town was hung by the neck before the door of the house where he was staying. The next day he embarked for Rhode Island, eventually returning to Boston, where he was again posted, and finally in June applied for readmission. He died suddenly in August of the same year.

James and Patrick McMasters were particularly offensive to the merchants. In 1770 Patrick was carted through the streets of Boston for persisting in his refusal to join the merchants, and this punishment was so roughly administered that, we are told, a woman viewing it died of fright (Essex Gazette, February 5, 1771). "I received a letter from Miss Cummings," wrote Mrs. Barnes, "which was far from being a cordial to my drooping spirits. She writes me word that one of the McMasters had been carted out of town at noonday in a most ignominious manner, and that the other two brothers had fled for their lives" (Letters of James Murray, Loyalist, pp. 177–178). The McMasters and others, finding public opinion against them in Boston, fled to Portsmouth, an event which roused a good deal of excitement there, and may have had something to do with Portsmouth's continued unwillingness to adopt non-importation.

[2] Committee to De Berdt, January 30, 1770, giving their version of the matter (Massachusetts Papers, pp. 132–135).

[3] "The True Sons of Liberty and supporters of non-importation are determined to resent any the least insult or menace offer'd to any one or more of the several committees appointed by the Body at Faneuil Hall, and chastise any one or more of them as they truly deserve; and will also support the printers in anything the

took place on March 5th, and the town was in an uproar and confusion. The Trade had to publish its determination to protect its own members and its printers from insult, and despite the colony act "establishing a watch for the safety and better securing the good order of the town of Boston," the police conditions were so lax that the populace did about as it pleased, defying court orders, destroying the houses of unpopular citizens and magistrates, tarring and feathering with impunity, gathering in crowds, pelting, jeering, and maltreating without interference. The situation reflects no credit upon the authorities of the town, whose citizens were zealous to do their duty only when fires were to be extinguished and patriotic enterprises executed.[1]

The non-importation movement was beginning to pass out of the hands of the merchants and into the control of those to whom trade was a secondary consideration. The Boston town meeting took up the question of how to strengthen the movement and appointed a committee for that purpose.[2] Again it entered on its records the names of those who continued to import, that posterity might know "who those persons were that preferred their little private advantage to the common interest of all the colonies," and again it offered, in burning and eloquent phrases, the thanks of the town to

committees shall desire them to print. ☞ As a warning to any one that shall affront as aforesaid, upon some information given, one of these Advertisements will be posted up at the Door or Dwelling House of the offender" (January, 1770, Massachusetts Historical Society, Broadsides).

[1] Remarks by Mr. Pierce in his introduction to John Rowe's Diary (2 Proceedings Massachusetts Historical Society, x. 57–58). The act mentioned empowered the selectmen of Boston to appoint thirty watchmen from among the inhabitants of the town, one of whom in each division was to be head or constable, and to keep an account of what was going on and to report to the selectmen once a week. The watchmen were to walk the rounds to prevent danger from fires and see that good order was kept. Any one resisting a watchman was to be fined not more than £5 or less than 40 shillings. The watchmen were authorized to call on any citizen for assistance, who in case of refusal was liable to a 40 shilling fine. The act was to be in force until 1770.

[2] Boston Record Commissioners' Reports, xviii. 12–13, 16, 20. The meeting expressed the hope "that the Patriotick Spirit so widely diffused, and so nobly ardent, uniting all parts of the Province and disposing them with Alacrity to aid one another upon all Occasions in the common cause, a Spirit not confined to [this colony] but extending to all the Colonies, will ensure by the blessing of Heaven the Prosperity of the whole, and soon produce a thorough, effectual, and permanent relief from our great and common Grievances" (March 16, 1770).

all who stood by the cause. John Rowe frankly expressed his dislike of the proceedings of the Body, thinking them "too severe," [1] and others were doubtless thinking the same. The partial repeal of the Townshend Act in April raised a new issue and the question arose as to whether the agreement should not be modified so as to admit all British goods except tea. The news of the repeal was known in Boston on April 24th and on the 30th a meeting of the Body was held, at which the merchants resolved to stand by the agreement and not to "send for any goods from Great Britain until the act imposing the duty on tea" should be repealed or until "the Trade in order to harmonize with the other colonies" should agree to alter such agreement. It still further enlarged the list of exemptions, adding certain articles that "we cannot at present manufacture in the province in so great quantities as we have occasion for at present." [2] On May 1st, the Salem town meeting, promising to support the agreement of the merchants, took up the question of the importers, who were making trouble there as well as in Boston. The next day, it forced John Appleton, Peter Frye, Abigail Epes, and Elizabeth Higginson to sign an agreement, in accordance with which their imported goods were to be stored under the direction of the

---

[1] He says this of the proceedings at the meetings of April 20 and 26. I have not been able to find the votes in question, but the call for the meeting on April 20 is as follows:

"To receive the report of the committee of inspection relative to the most unaccountable and extraordinary conduct of several persons who have imported goods contrary to agreement, particularly a Quantity of Tea; and to consider and determine upon some legal and spirited measures to prevent the nonimportation agreement being rendered abortive," etc. (Massachusetts Historical Society, Broadsides, April 20, 1770).

It will be noticed that the wording is the same as that of January 16th, except that the offence stated is different. Probably the meeting voted to deal more severely than ever with the offenders, who may be the same as those entered on the records of the town meeting of March 16th, and afterwards published by the merchants in the newspapers. See p. 244 note 1, below.

[2] Massachusetts Historical Society, O2517, no. 73. The' following articles were exempted: paper, glass, painters' colors, tacks, brads, nails of all sorts under 10 pennies, all kinds of utensils for carrying on any manufactures, lead, copper, "allum," grindstones, salt, coals, tinplates, hooks, lines, and other necessaries for the fishery, baize, duffils, hemp, duck, "ozenbrigs," fruit, oil, and all other kind of goods of the product and manufacture of any foreign ports in Europe usually imported from Great Britain, except any articles of luxury. This is a very different list from that of August 1, 1768.

committee of inspection.[1] Marblehead, Taunton, and other towns joined in this attempt to bolster up a failing cause.

VII

On May 26th, Newport broke the agreement into which she had entered on October 30, 1769. There had been from the beginning a great deal of intense feeling in the town on the subject of non-importation, and the disputes among the merchants had been long and heated.[2] So prolonged was the controversy that in October, 1769, the Boston merchants had said if Rhode Island did not come in they would treat her as the merchants of New York and Philadelphia had done and instruct their English correspondents to ship her no goods on penalty of losing the Boston trade.[3] Though both Providence and Newport agreed to non-importation in October of that year, the opinion prevailed generally that in the case of Newport the merchants were mainly Jews [4] and Tories with little enthusiasm for the cause. Rumors had come as early as May 9, 1770, that many of them were breaking the agreement and refusing to allow their goods to be stored, and very likely these rumors were true, for less than three weeks afterwards the break came. On the 26th the merchants voted to resume importation, and immediately sent letters notifying the others of the fact. Boston on the first rumor, having little confidence in Newport's sincerity, voted non-intercourse, and as the people of that town had not expressed a proper resentment at the action of the merchants, voted to break connection with them also.[5]

Philadelphia and New York followed suit. On May 23d the tradesmen and mechanics of the former city declared for non-intercourse, expressing "abhorrence" because of Newport's rumored

---

[1] Essex Gazette, May 8, 1770. The agreement is given in full in the Boston Gazette, October 8, 1770.

[2] New London Gazette, June 1, 1770.

[3] Boston Gazette, October 9, 1769.

[4] On the Jews in Newport, see Kohler, "The Jews in Newport" (Publications American Jewish Historical Society, 1897, no. 6, p. 69; no. 10, p. 11), where the number is given. See also Stiles, Literary Diary, i. 11; Itineraries and Correspondence, pp. 52–53. There was a Jewish Social Club in Newport in 1761 (Publications American Jewish Historical Society, iv. 58–60).

[5] Boston Gazette, May 28, 1770.

defection.[1] On May 30th, after the news had actually reached New York, a general meeting was held, not of the merchants, but of the Sons of Liberty, which denounced the Newporters as enemies of their country, voted to have nothing to do with them unless within a month they returned to their duty, and ordered all vessels from Rhode Island, lying in New York harbor, to depart within twenty-four hours. This action was, however, repudiated by the merchants, as the meeting had been called without the knowledge of the committee of inspection, which immediately resigned but was afterwards reëlected.[2] Connecticut, on June 1st, adopted resolutions similar to those of Boston.[3] Soon after, Hartford, New Haven, Marblehead, Elizabeth, New Brunswick, Baltimore, Annapolis, Wilmington, and Charles Town all declared in favor of non-intercourse with Newport and spoke with the utmost bitterness of that "dirty little colony of Rhode Island."[4] Newcastle, Wilmington

---

[1] New York Gazette and Weekly Mercury, May 28, 1770; Pennsylvania Chronicle, May 28, 1770; Pennsylvania Gazette, May 24, 1770; Boston Gazette, June 4, 1770. A Newport ship, Capt. Whitman, master, arrived in Philadelphia with a cargo, but was sent back.

[2] New York Gazette or Weekly Post Boy, May 28, June 4, 1770.

[3] New London Gazette, June 15, 1770. The same paper contains an elaborate account of four Connecticut traders, two from Hartford and two from Windham, who started immediately for Newport to take advantage of the leak.

[4] New York Gazette or Weekly Post Boy, June 11, August 13, 1770; Boston Gazette, June 25, 1770; Cape Fear Mercury, July 11, 1770; South Carolina Gazette, June 28, July 5, 1770. Ships were sent back from all these places. The resolutions adopted at a meeting of the inhabitants of Charles Town "at Liberty Tree," June 22, 1770, though too long to be printed here, are worthy of reproduction in part. They describe the Rhode Islanders as "dead to every feeling but a criminal attachment to their private interest," "betrayers of American Liberty," and guilty of "heinous duplicity of conduct." They class together the people of Georgia and Rhode Island as "deluded people" deserving "to be amputated from the rest of their Bretheren, as a rotten Part that might spread a dangerous Infection" (South Carolina Gazette, June 28, 1770).

Stephen Collins wrote to N. & R. Denison, June 8, 1770: "The people of Rhode Island have broaken through their agreement which I think they must resume again very soon, as the whole Continent are rais'd in just indignation against them, their produce being but little, their merchants depend on foreign trade chiefly and their vessels are almost every day drove out of one port or another on the Continent and not suffer'd to trade but carry their cargo back, so that I think where they gain a penny in the trade of dry goods, they will stand a chance of loosing a pound for want of their trade with the other colonies" (Collins Papers).

(Delaware), Chester, and other towns down the Delaware river took alarm and voted to have no dealings with the colony.[1]

This widespread vote of non-intercourse with Rhode Island showed either that to most colonial minds Newport was Rhode Island or else that the impression had got abroad that Providence also had departed from her agreement. This impression was partly true, for after the news of the partial repeal of the Townshend Act was known in America, some of the merchants of the city in May held a meeting and agreed to import all British goods except tea. Because of this, or because of a confounding of the two cities, several towns refused the vessels of Providence port entry and Windham published a spirited protest against her. This act angered the people of Providence, who considered themselves sufferers for the conduct of another town, and on May 31st they declared the decision of the merchants "too precipitate," renewed the old agreement, and passed a vote of censure against both Newport and Boston, resolving to purchase no goods from any one who imported into these towns contrary to the agreement. Newport replied, quoting the fable of the ass who kicked the lion, and citing instances where Providence herself had proved faithless. A writer in the Providence Gazette said:

The merchants of Newport broke through the agreement and were highly censured by the northern part of the colony. The town of Providence, 'tis well known, passed a vote of censure against them, which they affected to ridicule in a very awkward manner. 'Tis with pleasure, I observe, that none of the colonies have passed any censure upon this town in particular. This was reserved for the little, dirty, insignificant town of Windham, the inhabitants of which, without the least show of reason, have dared publicly to stigmatize a people, than whom none have been more zealous in supporting the cause of American liberty.

At an adjourned town meeting on June 6th, the merchants acquiesced in a majority vote for the old agreement and the old list of exemptions, and peace was once more restored.[2]

---

[1] News from Philadelphia, June 14 (South Carolina Gazette, July 12, 1770).

[2] Providence Gazette, May 26, June 30, 1770; Newport Mercury, June 4, 1770; New York Gazette or Weekly Post Boy, June 18, 1770; Staples, Annals of Providence, pp. 225–227. On September 5, 1770, Boston voted "That it appears to this Body that the town of Providence hath faithfully adhered to the non-importation agreement, and that all reports to the contrary are without foundation."

This exchange of amenities in the North found their counterpart in the South also, where the merchants of Georgia were apparently paying very little attention to their compact, and were continuing to import without regard to the obligation imposed upon them by their resolutions of September, 1769. They too were influenced by the partial repeal of the Townshend Act and considered their duty done when they excluded from their list of imports the single article, tea, the duty on which had not been removed. Probably this article was smuggled there as elsewhere from Amsterdam or St. Eustatius, so that to all intents and purposes the ports of Georgia throughout the period had been open to British goods. We know that her imports increased from £56,000 to £58,000 during the year 1769. To the Sons of Liberty of Charles Town this breach of faith was a sign of depravity. At the Liberty Tree meeting of September 27th, in denouncing the people of Rhode Island, they denounced those of Georgia also as having "acted a most singularly infamous part from the beginning of the present glorious struggle for the preservation of American liberties to this very instant," and because of their having basely taken "every possible advantage of the virtuous colonies" they voted to have nothing more to do with them.[1]

While thus Charles Town was expressing its opinion of Georgia, Newport of Providence, and Providence of Newport and Windham, and nearly all the colonies were breaking off intercourse with Rhode Island, Portsmouth was having its fling at Boston, and Albany at New York. The Portsmouth merchants had never adopted a non-intercourse agreement, and at this juncture were making extensive importations, which were not only exposed for sale, but were bought freely by the inhabitants of the town. At its meeting on May 25th, the Trade of Boston had resolved to have no intercourse with either the merchants or the inhabitants of Portsmouth, and had sent a letter to the former, urging them to change their attitude. But nothing was done, perhaps for the reason, as one of the Portsmouth people wrote to Boston, that they had no leader to direct public opinion.[2] A leader was to come, but not one favorable to the Boston proposal. On June 19, Patrick McMasters was "carted out" of Bos-

[1] South Carolina Gazette, June 28, 1770.

[2] South Carolina Gazette, July 12, 1770. Letter from Portsmouth to Boston, May 28, 1770, quoted in the South Carolina Gazette: "The merchants here have

ton and with his brothers fled to Portsmouth. The presence of the McMasters must have served to stiffen the town's determination to resist, for shortly afterwards the following notification was posted:

A number of people in the town of Boston have arrogantly published certain resolutions not to trade with this province. The total stopping of the coasting trade with Boston will directly advance the commercial and landed interest of the province. Every friend of the province will joyfully embrace the profer'd opportunity to assert his freedom and scorn all chains, even those forg'd in Boston.[1]

The position of Albany is somewhat obscure. Having entered the agreement in the summer of 1769, the merchants had remained outwardly faithful, although there is every reason to believe that Indian and other goods were imported by way of Quebec and Montreal, in disregard of the promises made to New York. Finally on May 18th, hearing that other colonies were "altering" their agreements, Albany decided to "alter" hers also, throwing open the trade to all goods, except tea. New York wrote on May 26th, expostulating so vigorously with the Albany merchants that they rescinded their action and went back to their former position. Naturally they were indignant when news came later of New York's decision to withdraw, and that too without consulting her sister colonies, and on August 7th the Albany merchants wrote a letter, expressing their opinion of New York in no uncertain terms.[2]

While the tide of success was thus ebbing in the outlying sections of the colonial area and discord was raising its ugly head among some of the individual towns, serious weaknesses were manifesting themselves in the very heart of the system itself. In New York and Philadelphia, as well as in Boston, the control of the movement was passing into the hands of the radicals, who under the designation of Sons of Liberty were demanding the continuation of the

received a letter from merchants in Boston on the affair of non-importation, but have not yet come to a final resolution. Happy should we be had we a generous Hancock to lead the way. . . . The inhabitants are friends to liberty but need powerful leaders."

[1] Rowe, Diary, June 19, 1770; Massachusetts Gazette, July 5, 1770; Adams, Annals of Portsmouth, pp. 226–227.

[2] New York Gazette and Weekly Mercury, August 20, November 8, 1770; New York Journal, August 23, 1770.

agreements in all their vigor. This radical party was composed of those who were poor and suffering, heavily in debt and in fear of the sheriff, of the typical frontier unrestrained element, spoiling for a mix-up and easily subject to crowd influences, of honest believers in the constitutional rights and liberties of the colonies and the "unalterable laws of nature," but with no interest in law or tradition or sympathy with the British colonial argument, and, lastly, of those who profited by smuggling and saw in the perpetuation of the movement a gain rather than a loss to themselves. In Boston and Philadelphia the conservative and radical forces acted more or less in combination, members of the merchant class being among the most active supporters of liberty and constitutional rights; in the smaller towns, where mercantile activities were ancillary to the dominant agricultural life, the radical or patriotic party was generally in control, while in the upper South — Maryland, Virginia, and North Carolina — the planters and lesser farmers were radical in sympathy, upholding the movement in the interest of American liberty and gradually forcing the moderates either to conform or to withdraw. In Charles Town the merchants and Sons of Liberty worked together in a fair degree of harmony, while in Georgia the conservatives seem to have been in control, for Jonathan Bryan and the few individuals excepted in the Charles Town vote of denunciation were unable to swing the movement in favor of prohibition. The test was now to come in the leading seaports. Would the radicals be able to maintain the agreements unaltered or would the conservatives win the day? In New York, where the decision was first reached, the two parties were well matched, the conservative merchants wishing to open the trade, the mechanics, tradesmen, retailers, and political radicals, aided by some of the merchants who had great influence with the populace, rejecting all compromise.

In both Philadelphia and New York, the repeal of the Townshend Act had been anticipated as early as November, 1769, and orders had been sent to England for the shipment of goods on condition that that event took place. During the winter the British merchants had gone ahead preparing goods for despatch to America, and the news of only a partial repeal came as a serious blow to them. They wrote letters to their correspondents in America saying that the failure of the total repeal was mortifying and exposed them to serious losses.

They hoped that the merchants, particularly those of Philadelphia, would enlarge their list of exemptions, and so keep the channel of trade open, or else would fall on some other method of saving them from "a melancholy situation." They informed their correspondents that goods were daily being shipped to Virginia, Maryland, Boston, Rhode Island, and Montreal, and would hence circulate through all the colonies, as the greater part were ordered by strangers unaccustomed to trade, and that unless the old merchants should order goods, the business would certainly find its way through a new channel.[1]

For these and other reasons, dissatisfaction found expression in Philadelphia early in 1770, and in April and May meetings of subscribers and importers were held in order to consider whether some alteration might not be made in the agreement. Many felt that the stagnation in business was unbearable and that the burden of suffering, not only within the city and province but also among the colonists at large, was unevenly distributed.[2] At a general meeting on May 14th, it was decided to send a letter to Boston, asking the merchants there how they felt about importation, and though in the meantime rumors spread that Rhode Island had defected and the New England merchants were secretly importing, the sentiment in Philadelphia was favorable to a strict adherence.[3] Final action was postponed until June 5th, when it was expected that replies would have been received from the other colonies, upon which a general and harmonious agreement might be based.

---

[1] Letters to Stephen Collins from Benj. & John Bowers, Manchester, February 1, 1770; William Neate, London, February 7, March 6, 26, 1770; Harford & Powell, February 28, 1770; Williams, Bellamy & Williams, London, March 1, 1770; Nath. & Robert Denison, Nottingham, March 8, 1770; and the many letters from Samuel Elam of Hull. Benj. & John Bowers wrote that they would be "very great sufferers," as "the greatest part of their fortune was expended in manufactures designed for the American market" (Collins Papers).

[2] Henry Drinker to Abel James, 1769–1770 (Pennsylvania Magazine, xiv. 43). See the letter of "Plebarius," in the Pennsylvania Gazette, May 24, 1770, suggesting a general subscription for the sufferers.

[3] Drinker wrote, May 26, 1770, that "notwithstanding the little dirty colony of Rhode Island had shamefully broken faith," yet this "flagrant violation and breach of their plighted honour" had not "staggered the merchants of New York or this place." In May "A Tradesman" wrote to the Pennsylvania Chronicle urging his brethren to enter into Resolutions denying their custom to any "who should dare an infraction of the mercantile resolutions."

On June 2d, the New York committee of inspection sent by express riders to New Brunswick, Elizabeth, and Perth Amboy, and to Philadelphia, Boston, and towns in Connecticut, letters signed by eighteen principal merchants, asking the recipients to collect as soon as possible the sentiments of their communities, whether to abide by the present agreement or to import at once everything except articles taxed. The committee also requested them to appoint six deputies each to meet at Norwalk on June 18th, for the purpose of exchanging opinions and of adopting "one solid system for the benefit of the whole, that no one colony may be liable to the censure or reproaches of another, but all share the same fate." [1] The request carried with it the undoubted hint that this "General Conference of the Merchants on the Continent" should vote to alter the agreement, and because of this fact it met with a cold reception. Though Connecticut at its meeting in Hartford [2] voted to send delegates, its committee of merchants reported against altering the agreement on the ground that a refusal to import tea, because affecting only the East India Company, which did not represent the English nation, would not influence in any way English manufacturers and would only serve to discourage friends, encourage the administration, and render futile any further associations in America. They were not impressed by the argument that as England had yielded in part so they were bound in honor to yield also, which was presented by their New York and Philadelphia brethren.

Boston's answer, drawn up at the meeting of the merchants on June 7, 1770, at which John Rowe and probably other merchants of conservative tendencies were not present, was a definite refusal of New York's request. It declared that the least alteration in the agreement would show "a levity of disposition probably injurious to the common cause," and that as Boston was only one of six maritime

---

[1] New York Gazette or Weekly Post Boy, July 2, 1770; New London Gazette, June 15, 1770.

[2] The Hartford meeting was held on June 1, so that there must have been an earlier letter, but I have not been able to trace it. It appears to have been written as early as May 16. There was a New York merchants' meeting on the 18th, but that was called to discuss non-importation, and deferred action, hoping the duty would be repealed (New York Gazette or Weekly Post Boy, May 21, 1770). An earlier letter from Connecticut was sent on May 19, replying to that from New York, and signed by Matthew Talcott, Richard Alsop, and Silas Deane (ibid. July 23, 1770).

towns in the province, she could not act without their advice and consent. At the same meeting the merchants voted non-intercourse with Portsmouth and, at this time or soon after, disclosed the spirit that was in them by posting the names of ten firms which were importing contrary to the agreement, and threatening all who traded with them.[1] Philadelphia also at its meeting on June 5th rejected New York's request and voted to adhere to the former agreements, and all the leading towns of New Jersey followed Philadelphia's example.

Thus rebuffed, the New York merchants proceeded with their plans. On Monday, June 11th, a number of merchants and mechanics waited on the committee of inspection, desiring that the sense of the city should be taken by subscription, whether to alter the agreement or not. A meeting was called the same evening, at which a form of ballot was drawn up and persons were appointed to circulate it. The question asked was, "Do you approve of a general importation of goods from Great Britain, except tea and other articles which are or may be subject to a duty on importation, or do you approve of our non-importation agreement continuing in the manner it now is?" The result of the canvass was believed to show a majority of votes favorable to alteration, and at once an advertisement was inserted in the papers and letters were despatched to Philadelphia and Boston, requesting their concurrence and saying that in case they did not agree, the sense of the town would again be taken.[2] This action of New York roused a storm of protest, not only from other colonies but also within the city itself. A meeting of the Sons of Liberty, led by Isaac Sears and Peter Vanderwort, registered a lively dissent, and both Boston and Philadelphia rejected the proposal absolutely.

[1] Boston Gazette, June 11, 1770; New York Gazette or Weekly Post Boy, June 25, 1770. The names are printed in a supplement to the Boston Gazette, June 18, 1770. They are John Gillespie, John Bernard, James McMasters, Patrick McMasters, Nathaniel Rogers, William Jackson, Theophilus Lillie, John Taylor, Ame and Elizabeth Cuming, Israel Williams & Son of Hatfield, and Henry Barnes of Marlborough. These firms had already been publicly entered in the town records on March 19, and may have been acted upon at the merchants' meeting of April 20, but I find no earlier publication in the newspapers.

[2] New York Gazette and Weekly Mercury, June 18, 1770. The members of the merchants' committee were Isaac Low, chairman, Henry Remsen, Jr., Jacob Walton, and J. H. Cruger. Isaac Low advertised in the Post Boy, November 26, 1770, that he had imported and that he had a right to do so and that he had certain goods for sale and hoped people would buy of him. A curious advertisement.

Returns from Connecticut and New York showed that the sentiment in those colonies was hotly in favor of the agreements.[1] Consequently, on July 9th, the New York merchants, acting on the terms of their letter, took a second vote, ward by ward, and when the result showed a victory for importation, they despatched their orders by the packet the Earl of Halifax, which by special arrangement with the postmaster was held to await the result of the voting, and these orders were for goods of every kind, except tea.[2]

New York's defection was a mortal blow to the cause and stirred the non-importing colonies to indignation and anger. It was the first permanent break in the system, for Newport, whose withdrawal in May had resulted in her commercial isolation, later reconsidered her action and returned to the fold. In New York city, the Sons of Liberty held meetings denouncing the merchants and declaring that not a pound's worth of goods, imported contrary to the agreement, should be allowed to land. They called the importers the "court party" and charged the chairman of the committee, Isaac Low, with being in the pay of England and truckling for office. They denied that the vote represented a majority of the citizens, in that only about a fourth took part, 1100 out of 4000, the remainder refraining from voting, thinking the proceedings irregular.[3] But the radicals, because of their violent methods, were rapidly losing their influence, and when in October the elections were held for city magistrates, they were defeated by a large majority.[4]

Outside of New York the verdict against the merchants' action was almost unanimous. The Philadelphians had a meeting at the State

[1] A letter to the Boston Gazette, June 25, 1770, gives the anti-merchants' point of view.

[2] New York Gazette or Weekly Post Boy, July 9, 16, 1770. See a very informing letter sent by Alexander Colden, postmaster, to Anthony Todd, secretary to the postmasters general in London, July 11, 1770 (New York Colonial Documents, viii. 218–221).

[3] New York Gazette or Weekly Post Boy, July 23, 1770. In a supplement to the paper appears a complete list of "alterers," returned by the ward committees to the committee of inspection. It distinguishes between "Importers," "Those zealous for Importing," and "Shop-keepers," and was printed to show that only about 800 were for importing, whereas there were probably 3000 whose votes ought to have been taken. In the list is the name of John Glover, Samuel Elam's agent in New York, whose letters throw light on the situation in the city at this time.

[4] Becker, op. cit., p. 93.

House on July 14th and passed reproachful resolutions, calling New York's decision a "sordid and wanton defection from the common cause," and voted to break off all commercial intercourse with her.[1] The inhabitants of Elizabeth, Woodbridge, and New Brunswick rapidly followed Philadelphia's example, hoping to cut loose from the commercial bondage to New York, as Portsmouth had hoped to do from Boston, and to set up an independent port at Perth Amboy.[2] The students at Nassau Hall, on July 13, on the tolling of the college bell, went in a procession to a place fronting the college and burnt the letter from New York at the hands of a hangman hired for the purpose.[3] On the arrival of the letter at Boston, the Body met, certain of the number marching to the hall in procession, with flags flying, upon one of which was inscribed "Liberty and no-importation," and there they "voted unanimously that the said letter, in just indignation, abhorrence, and detestation be forthwith torn into pieces and thrown to the winds as unworthy the least notice, which sentence was immediately executed." The breach in the body of the Boston merchants was now complete. Some of them attempted to prevent the procession, and John Rowe, blaming the bearer of the flag, declared that the meeting would prove "very prejudicial to the merchants and trade of the town of Boston." The Society had fallen under the control of the extremists, who wanted no compromise with Great Britain. This became evident when, a week later, the Body met and appointed a committee composed of John Hancock, Samuel Adams, Thomas Cushing, William Molineux, and others, to go to the northern towns, Salem, Marblehead, Haverhill, etc., whence rumors of importations had come, and see if these rumors were true. The committee was then to go southward to Providence and Newport.

---

[1] The protest is printed in the New York Gazette and Weekly Mercury, August 6, 1770.

[2] New Jersey Archives, xxvii. 202, 204, 206–207, 215, 218–219.

[3] Madison to his father, July 23, 1770 (Writings, 1900, i. 7; New York Gazette or Weekly Post Boy, July 16, 1770). At the Princeton Commencement Exercises, September 26, 1770, "Mr. *Ogden* defended this Proposition. *The Non-Importation Agreement reflects a Glory on the American Merchants, and was a noble Exertion of Self denial and public Spirit.* He was opposed by Mr. *Horton*, to whom Mr. *John Smith* replied." At the same exercises, "Mr. *Frelinghuysen* pronounced an Oration on the Utility of American Manufactures," and "In the Afternoon Mr. *Wilson* began an Oration on Commerce" (New Jersey Archives, xxvii. 268, 269).

The merchants of Salem and Newport were so angry at the news that they threatened to tar and feather the committee, on the ground that Molineux was an agitator and a nuisance, raising disturbances wherever he went. Nothing happened, however, and the committee, or certain members of it, made the visits northward and reported all satisfactory; and though on their southward journey they accomplished little at Providence, they persuaded Newport to renew her agreement, at a meeting on August 20th, Thomas Cranston, chairman, on the promise that Boston would intercede with the southern colonies to resume commercial intercourse with her. This Boston did, at the meeting held September 7th to hear the report of the committee, and as the first result of the letter despatched for the purpose, Philadelphia renewed soon after the old relations with Newport.[1]

Town after town followed in the wake of Philadelphia and Boston, denouncing the attitude of New York and severing commercial relations with her — Rye, Huntington, Hartford,[2] Norwich, New Haven,[3] Chesterfield, Mansfield, Hanover, Springfield, and Nottingham,[4] Burlington, Monmouth, and Sussex counties in New Jersey, Annapolis, Talbot county (Maryland),[5] and others. Already on June

---

[1] Rowe, Diary, July 24, 1770; Massachusetts Gazette, July 26, 1770; Boston Gazette, July 30, August 20, 27, September 4, 1770; New York Gazette and Weekly Mercury, August 17, 1770; New York Gazette or Weekly Post Boy, August 27, September 10, 24, 1770; Essex Gazette, August 28, 1770; Pennsylvania Gazette, September 20, 1770; Newport Historical Magazine, iii. 256.

[2] Boston Gazette, August 13, 20, 1770. "The gentleman-merchants of the committee in Connecticut, met at Hartford, Aug. 4, declared their abhorrence of New York, issued a card calling for a closing of all accounts with the merchants there, and on the 7th authorized the publishing of five names, William Bowes, Rufus Greene, Edward Church, Nathaniel Cary, and William Coffin, Jr." Their resolution declared that New York's act was "in downright violation of the solemn agreement of this colony and of the neighbouring provinces . . . an infamous breach of their public faith plighted to her sister colonies not to import, and is a practice so destructive to the natural and civil rights and liberties of the people of America, that we must hold New York . . . in the utmost detestation and abhorrence." This quotation illustrates the almost universal tendency to identify non-importation, at this time, with the constitutional claims.

[3] "The Plea of New Haven for Non-Importation," July 26, 1770, is printed from the Emmet Papers in the Bulletin of the New York Public Library, i. 184. It speaks of "our backsliding Brethren of New York, who have meanly prostituted the Common Cause to the present sordid prospect of a little Pelf." The meeting was presided over by Roger Sherman.

[4] Representatives from these five towns met at Mansfield and took action.

[5] Scharf, History of Maryland, i. 118–119, where the resolutions are given.

22d members of the House of Burgesses in Virginia had met with a body of merchants at Williamsburg and renewed the association;[1] on July 5th, the Sons of Liberty of North Carolina met at Wilmington, renewed their agreement, promised to sacrifice all intercourse with the West Indies, and to watch importations with care.[2] On August 22d, "a most respectable General Meeting of the Inhabitants" of South Carolina was held at the Liberty Tree, and denouncing New York's defection as "a scandalous revolt from the common cause of freedom and a bait to destroy every constitutional right," voted to break off all commercial intercourse with her.[3]

Among all the protests against the action of New York, none is more interesting and instructive than that of Connecticut, for it shows the attitude of a colony where mercantile interests played little part and where the predominant agricultural life was favorable to the cultivation of individualistic notions of human rights and liberties. The merchant-farmers of Hartford, Middletown, New Haven, Norwich, and Norwalk were ardent supporters of non-importation, a virtue that cost them little as they imported no goods directly from Great Britain. Connecticut had traded with Boston to 1750, when owing to certain currency acts of Massachusetts, deemed injurious and unjust, her merchants turned their trade to New York. But trade was always a subordinate issue in Connecticut, for whenever anything favorable to it was proposed in the general assembly, the farmers

[1] The Association of June 22, 1770, is differently worded in its preamble from that of May 18, 1769. It is less rhetorical and more businesslike in tone. The articles run about the same, except that the list of goods not to be imported is considerably altered. The Association is signed by Peyton Randolph for the burgesses and Andrew Sprowle of Gosport for the merchants (Virginia Gazette, June 28, 1770; New York Gazette and Weekly Mercury, July 23, 1770; Boston Gazette, July 23, 1770).

[2] Cape Fear Mercury, July 11, 1770; South Carolina Gazette, July 5, 26, August 9, 1770; New York Gazette or Weekly Post Boy; August 13, 1770. In reply to a letter from Charles Town, addressed to the Sons of Liberty of North Carolina, a committee, composed of members from Wilmington, New Hanover county, Bladen county, Duplin county, Onslow county, and Cumberland county, met at Wilmington. It took the members a long time to get together, as "the gentlemen lived long distances apart." Many of the merchants refused to sign the renewal.

[3] To the Sons of Liberty of Charles Town the New Yorkers were "traitors to their country, themselves, and ages yet unborn, who, no doubt, when groaning under a British yoke will forever curse the traitors" (South Carolina Gazette, August 16, 23, 1770; New Jersey Archives, xxvii. 293).

opposed such propositions as a scheme of the merchants, and incompatible with their interests. Many of the merchants themselves were farmers and landowners and to them non-importation was an advantage, as tending to raise the value of lands, increase the price of agricultural produce, and turn the balance of trade in their favor. Those who protested in Connecticut acted rather as landholders than merchants, and while keenly alive to their rights, they were also keenly alive to their profits. Importation, which was favorable to the merchants in the cities, was unfavorable to those who were farmers and landowners first and traders afterwards. Hence we have the most rhetorical and denunciatory resolutions from the country districts in Massachusetts, from the colonies of Connecticut and New Jersey, and from the planters of the South.

When news of what New York had done came to Connecticut, letters were sent to the principal trading towns of the colony, calling for a meeting of the merchants at New Haven, on September 13, 1770. The meeting was duly held, with Gurdon Saltonstall in the chair, and Silas Deane acting as clerk, and a series of elaborate resolutions was drafted, upholding non-importation, accepting again the long list of exemptions adopted the February before, and characterizing the defection of New York as a "precipitate desertion of the common cause of American liberty," and a violation of "reiterated solemn engagements with the other colonies, not only without their consent but in direct contradiction to their advice and entreaties." Then they voted to break off all intercourse with her.[1]

---

[1] Connecticut Courant, September 17, 1770. Just where Connecticut intended to purchase English goods is not clear. The merchants had broken with Boston, and now they broke with New York. New Haven, in its earlier non-importation agreement, voted to trade with Philadelphia and Boston, and probably in this case a return to the Boston connection was designed. "A Connecticut Farmer," writing to the New York Gazette and Weekly Mercury, August 27, 1770, urges the cutting loose from all connections and the opening up of direct trade with England. He wanted Connecticut to have her own trade just as the New Jersey towns were hoping to do. This cutting of new channels of trade was in the minds of the freeholders and inhabitants of Sussex county, New Jersey, a region of wheat, and iron and steel furnaces, who, in voting non-intercourse with New York, declared that they would send their wheat and iron by the "more natural and easy water carriage down the River Delaware to our friends at Trenton and Philadelphia." As early as 1738, Gov. Morris of New Jersey wrote to the Board of Trade: "They [the people] have warm desires and are big with hopes of carrying on a trade directly with Great Britain, instead of receiving Euro-

The New York merchants resented bitterly the attitude of the other colonies, but with no one were they so angry as with those of Boston, who had treated their letter with such scorn and indignity. They believed themselves to have been very strict in adhering to their agreement, and had greeted the information furnished by John Mein's pamphlet and sheets with something akin to consternation. In November and December, 1769, they became very uneasy lest Boston should not stand by her agreement and said that what John Mein was printing and what the merchants abroad were saying seemed to show that the merchants there were not acting with as much spirit and honesty as they themselves were. When Boston refused to coöperate with them in June, 1770, the New York committee replied that the refusal made a bad impression, for had the congress at Norwalk been held it might have had happy results, but rejected "gave so much discontent that numbers said it was only a scheme in you to continue importing under pompous resolves against it." [1] Though

pean commodities from their neighbors of Boston, New York, and Pennsylvania" (Colonial Office, 5: 973, F 31).

[1] New York Gazette and Weekly Mercury, October 15, 1770. New York said: "Can Carolina, Philadelphia, Albany, New Brunswick, Woodbridge, or New Haven, etc, still retain a desire to hold a union with these gentlemen [of Boston], though they promise ever so great a Union in Deceit? Can you still resolve and protest against the merchants in New York, who maintained their agreement inviolate, untill they were convinced of the propriety of an Alteration, and then acted bold and upright, publickly declaring their Intentions to the world — like Honest Men" (Massachusetts Gazette, October 4, 1770, supplement). For a Boston statement, see ibid. September 6, 1770, and note the following as a specimen of language used in Boston: "At this juncture, when the merchants of New York have shamefully violated the agreement and forsaken the cause of this country, — when those who wish to have the chains *fastened* upon us are assiduous in their endeavours to scatter the seeds of discord among the other colonies, — when they are casting the most *malicious aspersions* on the merchants of this town and province, and are artfully endeavouring to render them particularly odious in the eyes of the world, — when we feel the hand of oppression and tyranny daily growing more and more heavy upon us, — when the enemies of *America*, destitute of shame or remorse, insolently begin to laugh at her struggles for Freedom, and already flatter themselves that in a little time despotic power shall gain a complete triumph in a land of Liberty, — at such a time and under such circumstances everyone will judge it is the duty of each Individual in the community who loves his country to attend the public meetings — There to deliberate and consult with *candor*, to determine with *wisdom*, and to execute with that undaunted fortitude which becomes those only who are RESOLVED to be FREE." This statement was made at a meeting held in Faneuil Hall, and we are not surprised that it had to be adjourned because so few were present.

local conditions had their influence, and though the partial repeal of the Townshend Act played its part, yet the feeling that other seaports were breaking through their agreements rankled in the heart of the New York merchant. That goods were coming in by way of Boston, Philadelphia, and Annapolis, while the port of New York was tightly closed, was unbearable, and though the figures given and statements made in Mein's papers and the letters from England may not all have been true, the fact that the New York merchants believed them to be true is the main thing. They charged these cities with hypocrisy, and when the committee of inspection at Annapolis called the New Yorkers "rotten and treacherous," the latter retaliated by accusing the Annapolitans of clandestine trading and raising the prices of goods, and with having waited a year before taking action and then restricted their non-importation to but a few articles, an effort "untimely and feeble."

The Philadelphia merchants also became uneasy, as rumor after rumor came that Boston and other colonies were importing. They were told by a London correspondent that between Christmas, 1769, and June, 1770, £150,000 worth of goods had been sent to Boston, which seemed to show, as a writer to the Pennsylvania Gazette put it, that "the conduct of the Boston people was not as consistent as could be wished."[1] They were warned by another writer that the situation was one deserving to be carefully weighed by judicious merchants, especially by themselves, who had thus far "been duped by all the other provinces."[2] Stephen Collins, one of the most active of them at this time in urging alteration of the trade, believed the charges against Boston when he said, "The opening of the trade except in duty goods seems to be gaining ground fast and I think this province in perticular has been Deep'd [duped] long enough already, [and ought not] to suffer their Intrest to be sacreficed any longer;" and a little later he added, "I having on my part taken no small pains to bring it about, being highly suspicious that we were become the Dupe of some other colonies in the cause; which was fully evinced to

---

When the next meeting was held on September 5, a letter was voted to be sent to say that all the New York charges against Boston were "WITHOUT FOUNDATION" (Massachusetts Gazette, September 20, 1770).

[1] Pennsylvania Gazette, June 14, 1770.

[2] New York Gazette and Weekly Mercury, August 27, 1770.

me on my arival at Boston, where I was amas'd to see the Quantity of goods amongst them." To John Glover of New York he wrote, November 20th, "It seems as though I could not put up without seeing thee before thou goes to that Rebbel Town Boston, amongst them Deceitful, Canting Presbyterian Deacons."[1]

Under these circumstances, alteration in Philadelphia could not be long postponed. The manner in which it was effected can best be told in the "candid and true account" given in the letter of the committee of merchants, September 25th. After stating that the original agreement had been subscribed by only about 300, though "the rest of the inhabitants concurred in the measure so as to discountenance and discourage any attempts to violate it," and that for some time "the greatest harmony subsisted," the account proceeds:

The plan of non-importation not producing an immediate and total repeal of the act, some whose living and others whose prospects of gain depended on importing goods began to be uneasy under these restrictions. With them the members [seven in number] who had broken off from the committee associated. Sundry meetings were held, and in May last [1770], measures being previously concerted, a vigorous push was made to break the agreement entered into. The voice of the public which was against them, and some concurring circumstances prevented them from carrying their design at the time, but the defection of New York, which followed soon after, giving them fresh spirits, they rallied again, and having secretly concerted a plan, they got a paper drawn up, signed by themselves and seven others, which they presented to the chairman of the committee on the eve of the 12th inst. [September], and because the committee would not comply with their proposal which was contrary to the non-importation agreement, the gentlemen themselves, without consulting the committee, ordered notices to be sent around to call a general meeting of the subscribers at D[avenport]'s tavern, in order that none but subscribers might be present. A number of subscribers refused to come, but the committee was present.[2]

The meeting was held on September 24th, with Thomas Willing in the chair. Voting down three substitute motions, to consult the other colonies, to adopt the Maryland and Virginia forms of non-importa-

---

[1] Letters to Samuel Elam and William Neate, November 24, 1770, and to John Glover, November 20, 1770 (Collins Papers).

[2] Pennsylvania Gazette, October 4, 1770.

tion, or to adopt the same provided New York and Boston would agree, and refusing to submit the question to the inhabitants of the city, the subscribers carried through a resolution to alter the agreement and to open the trade in all but tea and other dutiable articles.[1] This action of the subscribers called out indignant protests from the people of Philadelphia and the neighborhood, and a meeting was called at the State House on the 27th, with Joseph Fox as chairman, which deprecated the hasty action of the "importers of dry goods" and recommended the acceptance of an agreement like that of Maryland. Though the merchants immediately despatched orders to England, the feeling against them was so strong in the city, that even in November there was some doubt as to whether consignments could be safely received.[2] But with goods coming in by way of New York and Maryland, the Philadelphians could not hold out, and before November was over the port was open for all but the dutiable articles.[3]

---

[1] Pennsylvania Gazette, October 4, 1770; New York Gazette or Weekly Post Boy, October 1, 1770. Capt. Bosley wrote to Collins: "Last Thursday was a meeting of the subscribers to the non-importation agreement at Davenport's. J. Gibson spoke much and I am told very well against the trade being opened; W. West spoke strainously on the other side and gained the point. They are now making out their orders to go by the London packet, Capt. Cook" (Collins Papers).

[2] Many London merchants had sent goods to Philadelphia in August and September, hoping the trade would be opened. Samuel Elam of Hull loaded the ship Commerce in August with bales for both New York and Philadelphia, and consigned them to John Glover, New York. Glover had a great deal of trouble with this consignment, for it was not until November that Philadelphia merchants dared receive their bales. Some of the Philadelphia consignees were Geo. Emlin, Abraham Usher, Joseph Swift, Benj. Wynkoop, Isaac & Joseph Paschall, Jacob Winey, James & Drinker, William Wisher, Richard Parker, Thomas Clifford & Son, John & Clem Biddle, Matthias Aspden, John Steinmetz, Caleb & Amos Foulke, and Stephen Collins. All wrote Glover in November to forward by the Bordentown stage, to be deposited at the Crooked Billet tavern. "I believe none will hinder their coming," wrote Parker. "Do not apprehend there will be any difficulty in receiving of them," wrote the Cliffords. As it happened, the Commerce was wrecked off the Maryland coast, November 11, and though 400 bales were saved they were so much damaged that they had to be sold at public vendue in New York (Collins Papers; New York Gazette and Weekly Mercury, December 3, 1770).

[3] "Goods are dayley arriving here from New York," wrote C. & A. Foulke, November 15; "I find great quantities of goods are coming here from Maryland," B. Wynkoop, November 10; "I have an assortment of broadcloths coming by

Just as the news from New York aroused the subscribers of Philadelphia, so the news from New York and Philadelphia aroused the merchants of Boston. The meetings of the Club at Mrs. Cordis's were very frequent in September and John Rowe was present at nearly all of them. He was also present at the General Meeting on September 15th, when the decision was reached to send a letter to Philadelphia proposing a "meeting of committees from the neighboring colonies," the very thing that the Boston merchants had rejected so vehemently when New York suggested it in June. Manifestly the moderates, who had not approved of the proceedings of the Body in the summer of 1770, were once more in control, and the agitators were losing credit in Boston as they were doing in New York at the same time.[1] But the decision of September 15th came too late, The Philadelphia merchants had already made up their minds to alter the agreement and hope of united action was no longer possible. Although Salem made a last effort to uphold non-importation,[2] the end had come. When the circular letter arrived from Philadelphia, there could be no longer doubt as to what Boston would do. On October 11th the Body met at the Coffee House and unanimously voted to accept the inevitable, by altering the agreement and opening the ports to all goods from Great Britain, except tea. On the 18th all stored articles were returned to their owners.

Providence, Marblehead, and Salem followed, and advertisements began to appear in the papers of prohibited goods exhibited for sale,

---

way of Maryland, which will be sufficient for my spring sale," Abraham Usher, November 29 (Letters to John Glover).

[1] This is inferred from the names of the members present (Rowe, Letters and Diary, pp. 206–207.)

[2] A meeting was held in Salem in September to denounce the "infamous conduct" of the four importers (p. 235, above) who had signed the agreement of May 2, 1770, and on September 22 had broken it by taking their goods out of storage, "breaking open the stores with force and violence, armed with a process of law, and assisted by the under-sheriff." The meeting voted to boycott the stores and shops of the four, and even the truckman who handled the goods. A narrative of the circumstances, a terrible piece of thunder, is given in the Essex Gazette, October 2, 1770. Peter Frye, one of the offenders, wrote a letter defending himself, and saying that there were so many leaks everywhere, at Marblehead, Portsmouth, and Boston, that he was justified in seizing his property and offering it for sale. In the Essex Gazette of the 9th are published the names of three persons who had purchased goods of the four (Boston Gazette, October 8, 1770; Essex Gazette, October 2, 9, 1770).

"by leave of the committee of inspection."[1] Salem was selling articles "imported in the last ships from London" in December; glass, paper, and painters' colors were freely offered, and by the opening of the new year trade was in full swing, somewhat to the embarrassment of the English merchants, one of whom wrote, "The Boston trade coming at the heel of the Philadelphia trade has been of some inconvenience to us."[2] That Boston's action caused surprise and some consternation in New England, we can well believe. Said one writer: "From the borders of Connecticut all the way to Boston, you will find people in every town exclaiming against Boston, for imposing upon the country, by false representations and drawing them into measures which they say will ruin the province;" and John Temple could speak of that "unfortunate & (I could wish) ever to be forgotten year 1770 when with everything at stake, they threw up the important game when they had all the trumps in their own hands & like a Spaniel meanly cringed & kiss'd the rod that whip'd them."[3]

With the northern ports open from Portsmouth to the Delaware, the southern colonies could not long hold out. The merchants of Baltimore recommended alteration at a meeting in that town on October 5th, but at a general convention at Annapolis, three weeks later, the Baltimore suggestion was thrown out and a vote to adhere was adopted. No further action appears to have been taken, but after the news from Boston arrived, all attempts to uphold the agreement seem to have been given up. Of formal alteration in Virginia,[4] North Carolina,[5] and Georgia we have no sign, but at Charles Town,

---

[1] Essex Gazette, November 20, 1770.

[2] Denison Bros. to Collins, January 10, 1771.

[3] Boston Gazette, December 24, 1770; 6 Massachusetts Historical Collections, ix. 284.

[4] Virginia was one of the last, if not the very last, to give in. Perkins, Buchanan & Brown wrote to Thomas Adams, April 9, 1770: "The duty on Tea is yet retained, the repealing the other three articles certainly does not redress the grievance North America complained of. This being the case surely your resolution of May 18 should be strictly observed" (Virginia Historical Society, File 5). Just when action was taken I have not discovered, but it was not until after June 1, 1771, for on that date Jefferson wrote from Monticello to Adams, "The day appointed for the meeting of the associates is not yet arrived, but it seems certain that the restrictions will be taken off everything but the dutied articles" (Jefferson, Writings, i. 387).

[5] Regarding the situation in North Carolina, James Iredell wrote in October,

after intelligence had been received of the departure of most of the northern colonies from their resolutions, a general meeting of the inhabitants was held at the Liberty Tree on December 13th, with Henry Laurens in the chair. After much silence and hesitation a "breaking through" motion was carried. Tea was barred, luxuries discouraged, and local manufactures upheld, but otherwise business returned to its former freedom. On the 27th, all British goods held in confinement were released and given back to their owners. So ill-content were the South Carolinians with the conduct of the northern colonies, that it was with difficulty a vote was defeated declaring for commercial non-intercourse with them, and the printer of the Gazette probably expressed a general feeling when he wrote:

They are restrained by only one Consideration, that the Defection not having been among the *Landholders, Farmers,* and *Mechanicks,* who are perhaps, in general, as well affected to the just Rights and Liberties of America, as ourselves, it would be unjust to retaliate upon *them,* for the Injuries received from *some* of the *Merchants* of those Colonies. It must, however, be acknowledged, that the Trade with those Colonies is far from being *beneficial* to this; that except for *Bar Iron, Sheep,* and *Oil,* we might supply ourselves with almost every other article imported thence at Home, by proper attention and encouragement; and that they drain from us our Specie and mostly for mere Trash.[1]

With this somewhat ungenerous fling at the northern colonies, the second movement for the non-importation of British goods came to an end, and, as another southern writer said about the same time, "The so much boasted patriotism of non-importation throughout the colonies seems likely to terminate in nothing worse than to deprive the ladies of a dish of tea."

Thus the non-importation movement which had succeeded so well in 1765 and had been renewed with such enthusiasm in 1768–1769, came to a somewhat untimely end. It had not been a failure, for it was to no inconsiderable extent responsible for the removal of the duties on glass, paper, lead, and painters' colors, but it failed to effect the repeal of the acts of 1764, 1765, and 1766 and the removal of the

1771, "All mobbing is at an end here and we are once more at peace" (McRee, Life of Iredell, i. 93).

[1] South Carolina Gazette, December 13, 27, 1770.

duty on tea, and it accomplished nothing whatever in the effort to obtain British recognition of the constitutional claims of the colonies. Primarily it came to an end because the merchants in New York and elsewhere were satisfied with the partial repeal of the duties, and were unwilling to undergo further losses for the sake of tea and a constitutional claim which had nothing to do with trade. And there were other reasons which may be briefly summarized.

Before the movement was fairly under way, it began to show serious structural weaknesses. The merchants and importers were divided among themselves, not only on the original question but even more on the place of the movement in the struggle for liberty and self-government. The retailers and tradesmen, possessed of small capitals, found themselves unable to do business, and were threatened with the loss of their trade and consequent ruin. The people at large, to whom non-importation was a matter not of the pocket-book but only of self-denial, due to scarcity and high prices, were antagonistic to the merchant and charged them with preferring gain to patriotism and love of country. The radicals and agitators, irresponsible in thought and action, often added fuel to the flame of discord, and with little to lose engaged in acts of persecution against those who dared to oppose them.

In the system itself there were many defects. The colonies were not united on a common plan. Some were importing without restraint. Others were admitting everything except a few articles. Others again were putting an entire stop to their trade. There could be no firm union where men differed so widely and complained so bitterly. The agreements of the tobacco colonies allowed entrance to articles that were barred in the North. All the southern colonies admitted Indian goods that were so essential to Albany's prosperity, yet Albany, blocked by New York, could legally get none at all. There was a constant tendency to adjust the lists of exemptions, which even in the North were drafted according to local needs and preferences. The importers of dry goods, whose business was standing still, complained of the importers of wines and molasses, who had greater opportunities for profit. Maryland admitted slaves which were excluded elsewhere in the South. Where the agreements were the work of others than the merchants, the latter took umbrage at the voting away of their property by those who were not concerned with trade, and refused to

99

submit, a fact seemingly true of Georgia and in a measure true of North and South Carolina also. Many merchants yielded to pressure from England, where shipowners and exporters became restless as their ships lay idle and bent their efforts, often unconsciously, in favor of resumption.

As the movement progressed, the seaports and larger towns were divided into antagonistic and often hostile groups. Laurens speaks of the "squabbles" in Charles Town, about "resolutions, subscriptions, and non-subscribers," etc. "Much too much has been said on both sides," he wrote, "for the parties have left the subject upon which they began to contend and are harrowing each others private characters." The inland towns, to which imports were in themselves but a trifling consideration, found ample opportunity to reprimand the mercantile centres for their lukewarmness to the cause of liberty. The larger towns accused each other of unfaithfulness and hypocrisy, and newspaper writers, in language far too full of calumny and innuendo, engaged in controversy, circulating suspicions without proofs, and making assertions that were sometimes designed to convey false impressions. James Bowdoin expressed surprise that the agreements had "continued so long, for besides the operation of interest there were the underworking and lies of emissaries to make [the colonies] jealous and diffident of each other."

Apart from the psychological aspects of the situation, consideration must be given to the impracticability of non-importation itself. Commerce, like water seeking a lower level, finds its way despite obstacles, and if one channel is closed makes another. Though the imports of New England, New York, and Pennsylvania fell off heavily in the year 1769, so much so that the British merchants complained of their losses and the total balance of trade approached an equilibrium, those of Canada and the Carolinas increased by a third and those of Maryland, Virginia, and Georgia by a small but perceptible fraction. Enlarged demands from Russia and other parts of the European continent lightened somewhat the burden of the British merchants, but there were many who, alarmed for the security of their property and fearing a colonial repudiation of debts, sought entrance for their goods into America. Though many cargoes were turned back, others broke through, either by old or by new channels. Quebec and Montreal became loopholes for Albany and New York; Portsmouth, Casco Bay, and Falmouth admitted goods for New England; Cape May was a landing place for Philadelphia; and importations for New York and Philadelphia came in through Maryland and Virginia. No coast line can be completely sealed against the admission of necessary though prohibited goods.

The non-importation movement began as a merchant's device wherewith to obtain a redress of trade grievances; it ended as an instrument in the hands of political agitators and radicals for the enforcement of their claims of constitutional liberty and freedom. Had it been directed by the merchants and conservatives alone, it would undoubtedly have accomplished its purpose, as it did at the time of the Stamp Act; but when wielded by the extremists, it broke under the strain, because those who obtained control of it lost sight of its original object and in admitting no compromise, attempted the impossible.